AF326599

Unspoken Gift
Candy Waters Autism Artist

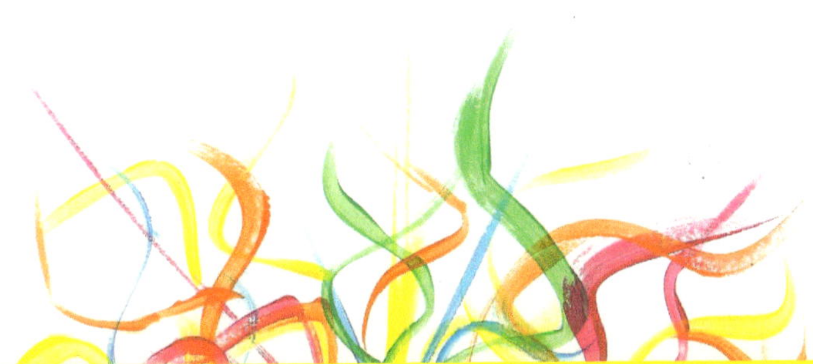

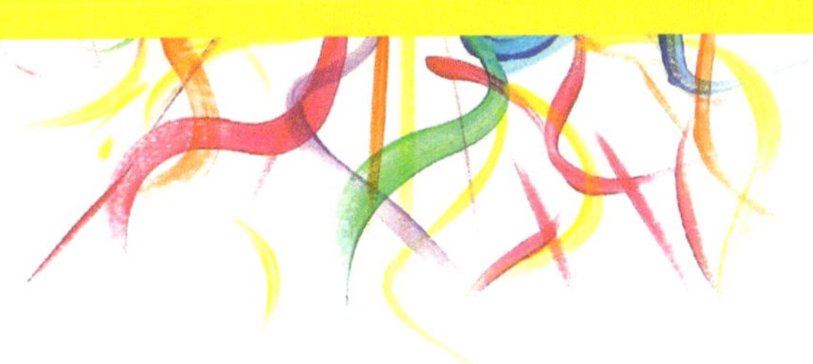

"This book is to share the voice of Candy through her artwork, please take note of her expressions and how her progress changes over time and we want to encourage parents everywhere to embrace their child's unique talents."

Unspoken Gift

Candy Waters Autism Artist

TABLE OF CONTENTS

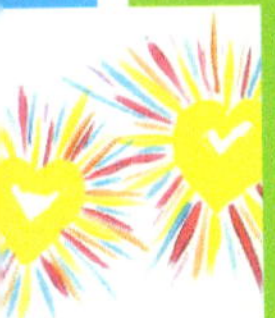

- Introduction
  The Art of Candy Waters
- Foreword
- Appendix
- Candy's Fans Speak
- Acknowledgements
- Candy's Famous Fans

"Candy Waters' art book is yet another example of the talent that lies within the untapped minds of those who live with autism. Candy's art is her unspoken gift to all of us"
~ Joe Mantegna

The Art of Candy Waters

We would like to tell you about our daughter Candy Waters, the artist featured in this book, *Unspoken Gift*. Candy is a beautiful redheaded 16 year old girl who is nonverbal and has autism. Although Candy cannot communicate with words, she is able to speak to the world through her art.

When Candy was born she had bright red hair and she looked like a little strawberry shortcake doll that was absolutely beautiful and perfect. Like all normal children, Candy soon began talking and pointing at things around her but by the age of three she lost these abilities. This led to her being diagnosed with severe autism. Her doctors told us that Candy would need life-long care. This was devastating! In the midst of that emotional devastation, had anyone said to us that Candy would one day become a famous artist, we would have thought they were crazy.

Candy was six years old when the executive director of an autism school in Chicago asked us if our daughter could paint a picture for a fundraising event she was organizing for the school. We were not sure Candy could paint. Autism had affected her fine motor skills and we had not experimented with having her paint, but we decided to have her try for the sake of the event. To our amazement, Candy began to paint and, best of all, she looked happy! Her first creation was something that looked like a sun. She had always loved being outdoors and since she was a baby we had sung a children's song to her called *Mr. Sun* so the painting was a natural progression.

At the art gallery where the school fundraiser was being held, Candy's Sun painting sold for $100! We were ecstatic! People liked Candy's art! One couldn't help but notice, too, that as Candy painted she was visibly happy, so it was no decision at all to help her continue to paint. Then, in the summer of 2013, Candy's *Mr. Sun* painting was selected to appear on the cover of The University of Irvine California (UIC) magazine's summer issue and Candy's art career took off.

We like to say that Candy doesn't paint with her hands—she paints with her heart and soul. Through Candy's art, she is giving us glimpses into her world allowing us to see what she sees and feel what she feels. Truly, Candy's world seems like a beautiful, happy place. We believe that her art inspires other people with autism to follow their dreams and helps parents of autistic children to understand that their child also has the potential to create no matter where he or she is on the autism spectrum.

Painting has been very therapeutic for Candy improving her fine motor skills as it brings her joy. Our artist daughter has a very unique, colorful, happy style of painting. She seems to have a perfect sense of how colors blend. Many artists say that painting is poetry and poetry is painting but with words. Candy simply paints pure poetry. Candy's art and her story have helped to increase autism awareness nationally and internationally. Also, it helps to find support for your family when you have a child with autism. One of the great autism organizations that helped our family so much is Autism Speaks.

We never force Candy to paint; we let this happen organically. We keep Candy's brushes in one special place so that when she picks up a brush and sits herself down where she wishes to paint, we know it's time to set up her art supplies.

Just to mention some of the recognition Candy's work has generated:
Candy's Mr. Sun paintings are featured regularly on CBS Sunday Morning. Another painting, *Ray of Hope*, is displayed in the newly constructed Dan Marino Foundation's the Marino Campus located in Fort Lauderdale, Florida. Another—*Pure Consciousness*—is on display at the main office of the David Lynch Foundation in New York City, New York. Also, a post of Candy's painting has gone viral on Facebook with 500,000+ Shares. Numerous news segments and articles have appeared in print and on television about Candy and her art. One of Candy's Sun paintings is prominently displayed in Park Ridge, Illinois City Hall. Hometown of two famous ladies. Democratic Presidential Candidate Hillary Rodham Clinton and Artist Candy Waters.

Candy's many fans include celebrities and her Facebook page has 100,000+ Likes from around the world. The David Lynch Foundation which teaches Transcendental Meditation (TM) provided us her parents with the technique that helps us cope with the stress of living with autism. Because of this our dream is to one day see an original *Candy Sun* painting in every TM Center worldwide. We even dare to dream that one day Candy's art will be on exhibit at The Art Institute of Chicago.

Children who have autism can achieve wonderful things no matter where they are on the autism spectrum. Our job as parents and caregivers is to help them find what allows them to best express themselves and enable them to work it to their best advantage. And, although this is true for all disabilities, we like to say, "Where words fail, music and art speak. Music and art are a must for autism." In fact, our friend Chicago actor Joe Mantegna has said, "Candy Waters art book is yet another example of the talent that lies within the untapped minds of those who live with autism. Candy's art is her unspoken gift to all of us." Mantegna's daughter Mia also has autism and paints. So, our advice to other parents of a child on the autism spectrum is to never give up faith, love and hope.

Thank you and enjoy looking at our daughter's work.

Faith, Love and Hope,
Robert and Sandy Waters—Candy's proud Mom and Dad

FOREWORD

by Anna Kennedy OBE (Officer of the Order of the British Empire)

I am honored to be asked to write the foreword to Candy's Art Book. I have followed Candy's Art and spoken on many occasion's to Sandy her Mum over the last few years through the power of social media.

It was also a privilege to receive a wonderful sunshine painting from Candy to display at "Autism's Got Talent" show in London and at our school in Kent. Candy very much reminds me of my son Angelo who also is on the Autism Spectrum. My eldest son Patrick has a diagnosis of Asperger's Syndrome and both my boys are at different ends of the Autism Spectrum.

My son's have taught me so much and we get through different challenges everyday together some days good some days not so good. It never fails to touch my heart to see the fantastic talent that is out there within the Autism Community hence our showcase of performers and art work in central London of "Autism's Got Talent" which is in its fifth year.

Looking at Candy's Artwork always gives me such enormous pleasure. She is helping to spread the important word and communicating through every stroke of her brush about the wonderful creativity that is so often denied the opportunity to shine and be heard around the world.

I would like to wish Candy all the luck in the world with her new art book and am proud to be a small part of it.

~Anna Kennedy OBE (Officer of the Order of the British Empire), Autism Mum & Autism Activist

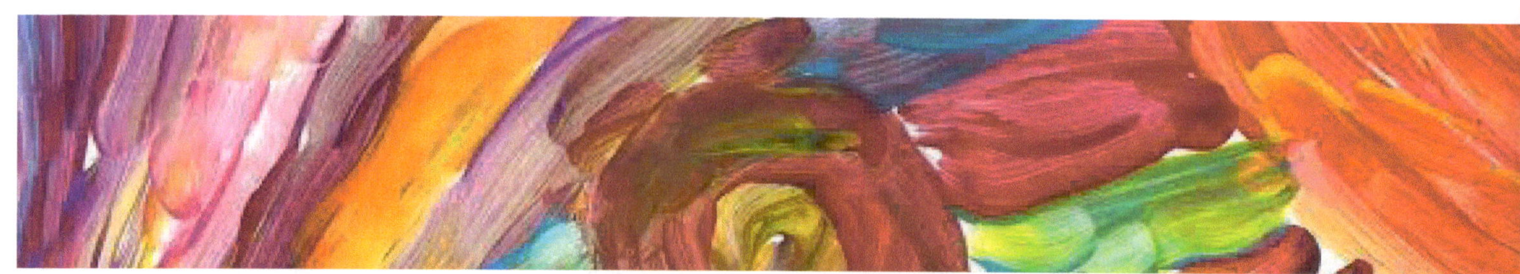

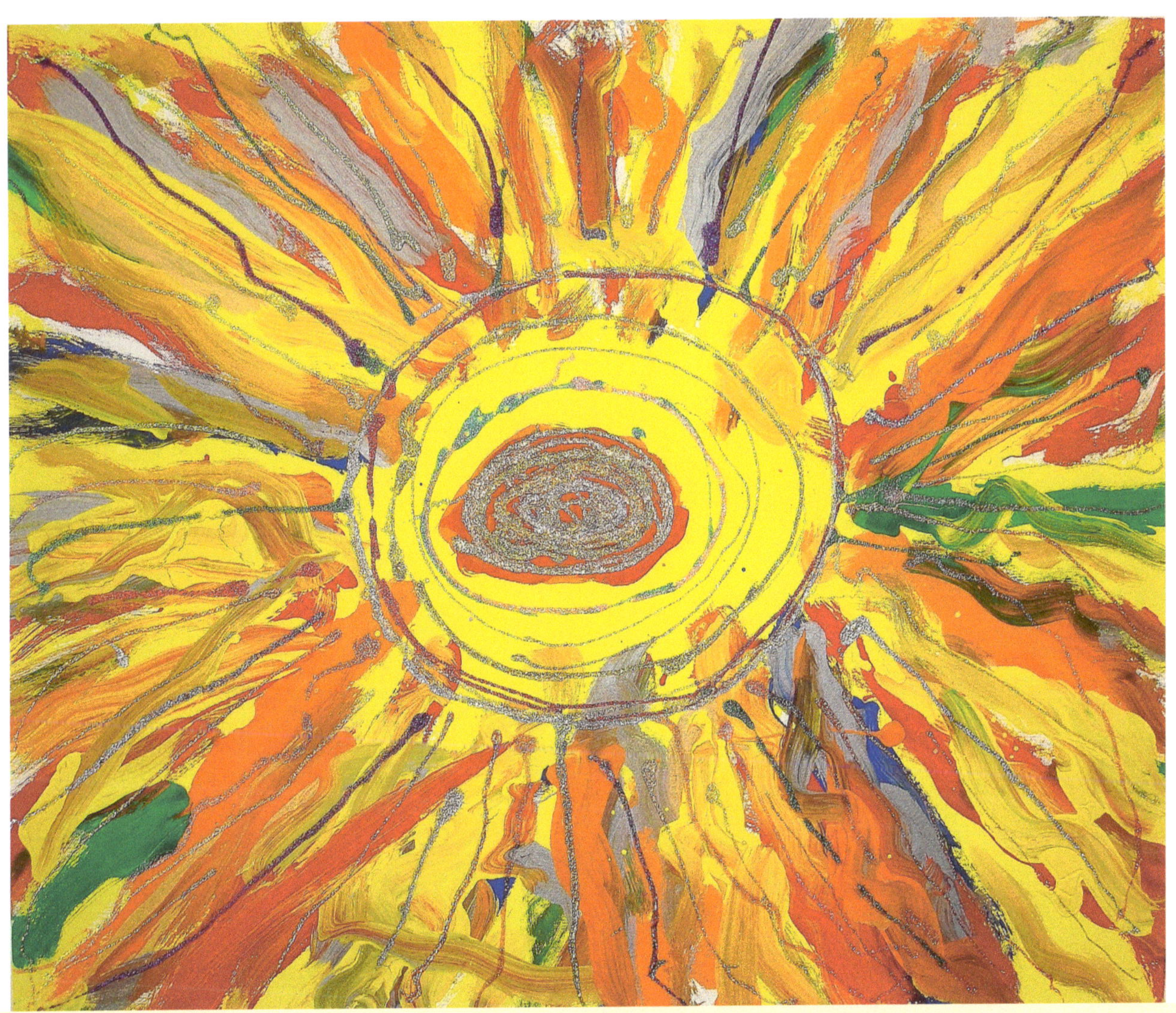

Mr. Sun

Date completed: November 8th, 2007

This painting is one of the first paintings that Candy did. We always sang the song Mr. Sun to Candy and this piece reminded us of that.

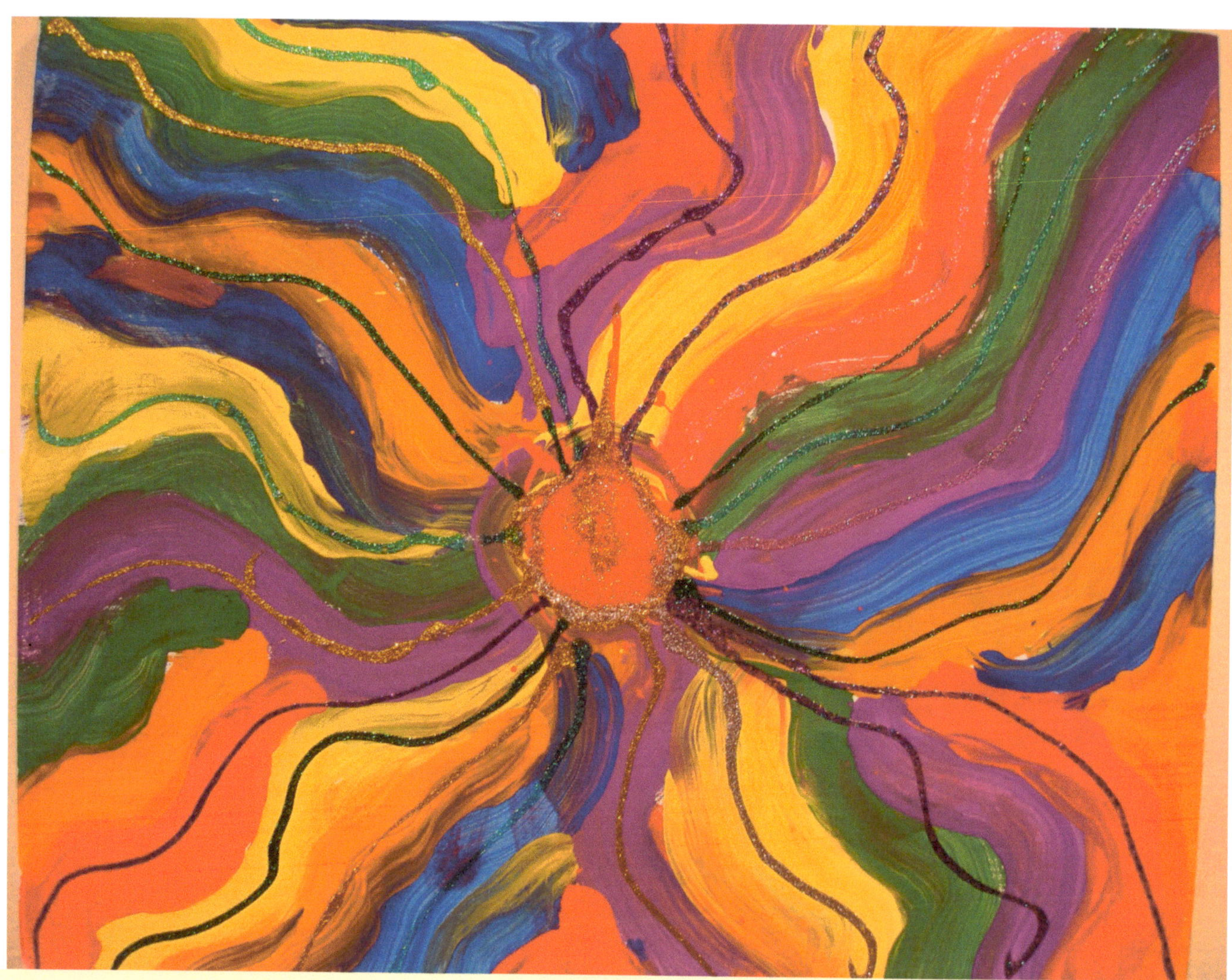

Rainbow Sun

Date completed: October 5th, 2008
This is an early painting by Candy.

Butterflies

Candy loves seeing butterflies flying. When she sees one in the yard she stops what she is doing to watch. Candy is so in tune with nature.

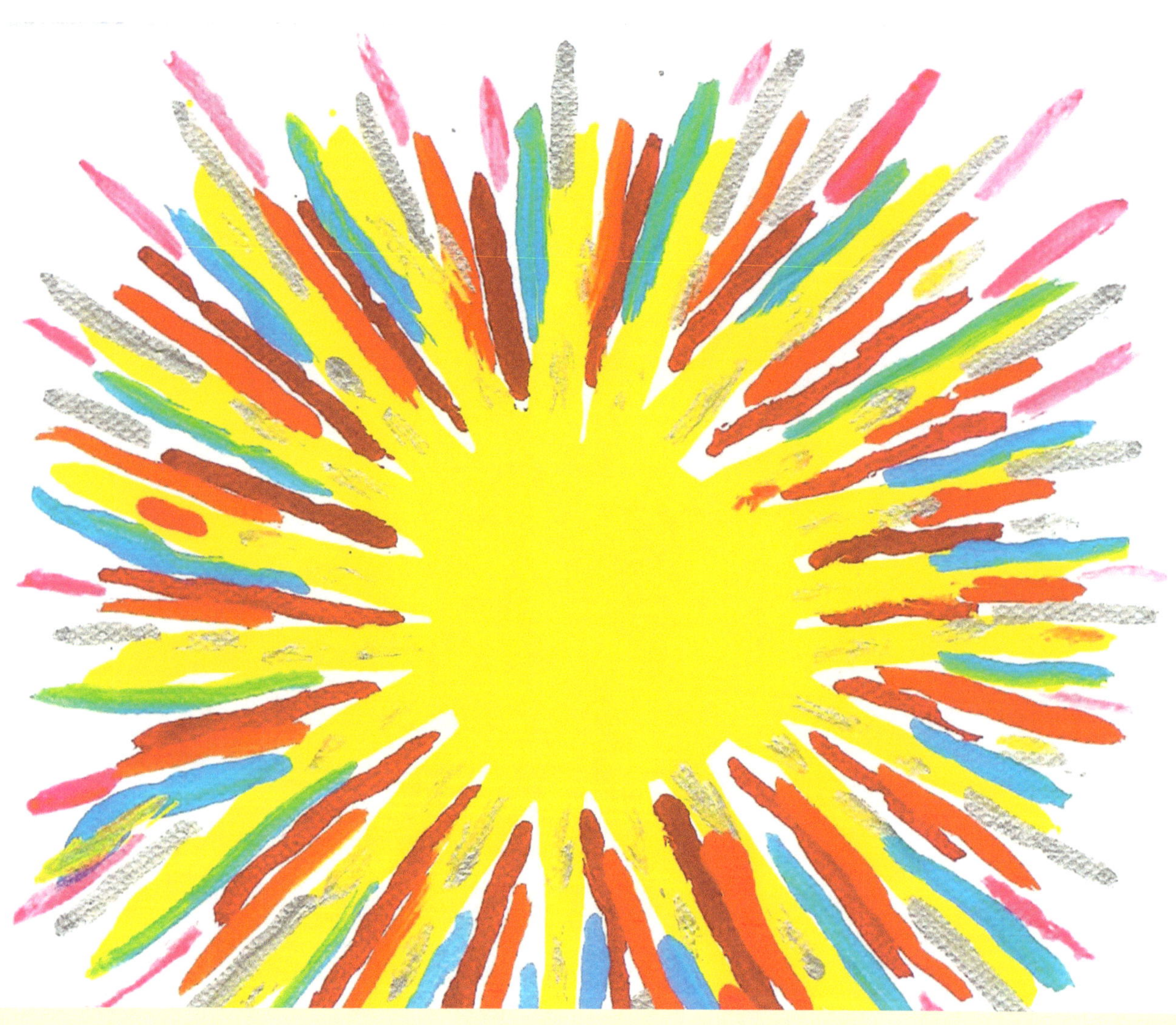

Boom

Date completed: June 27th, 2010
Candy enjoyed painting this piece. Painting is
therapeutic and helps Candy focus.

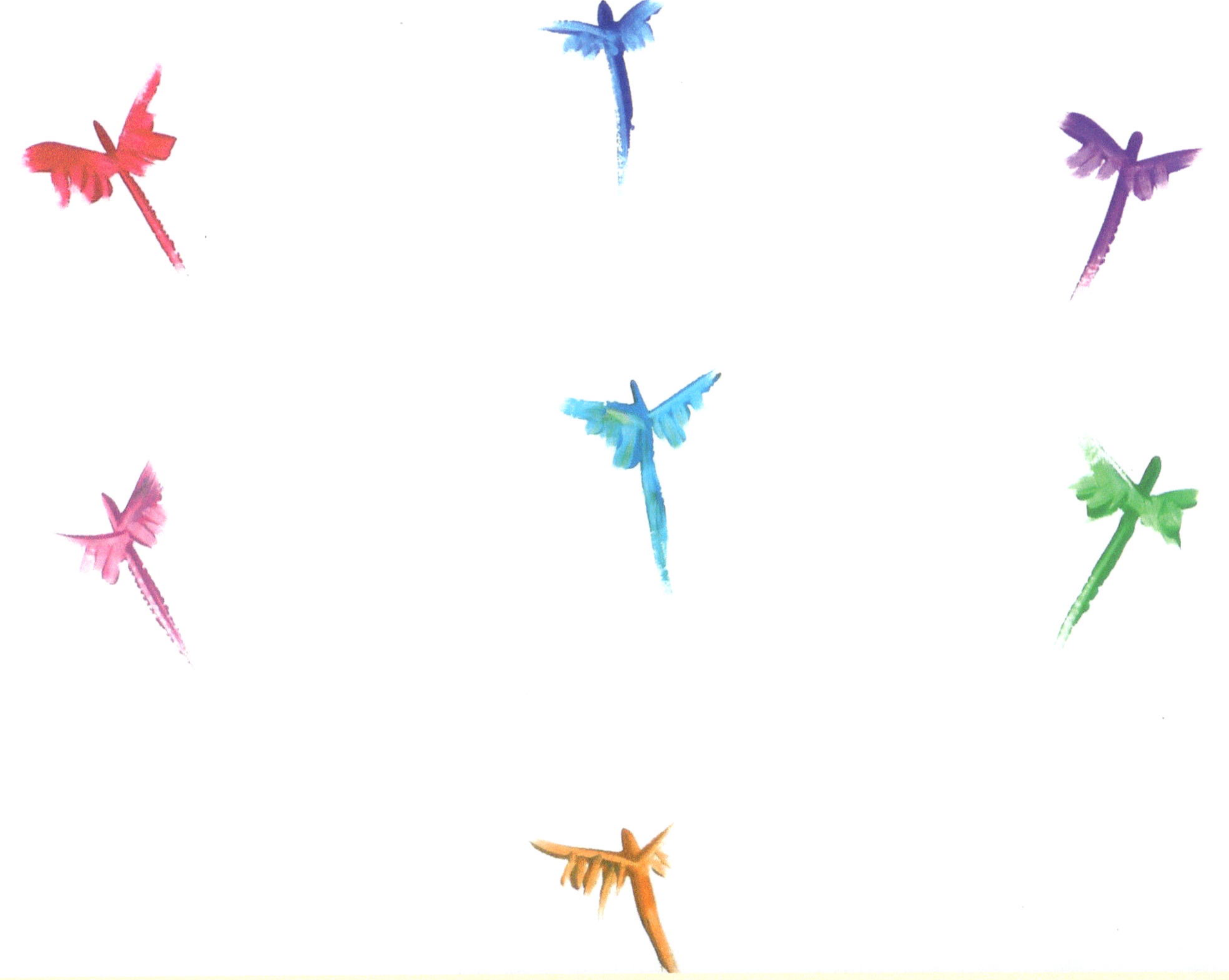

Rapture

Date painted: July 14th, 2010
Candy painted this outside.

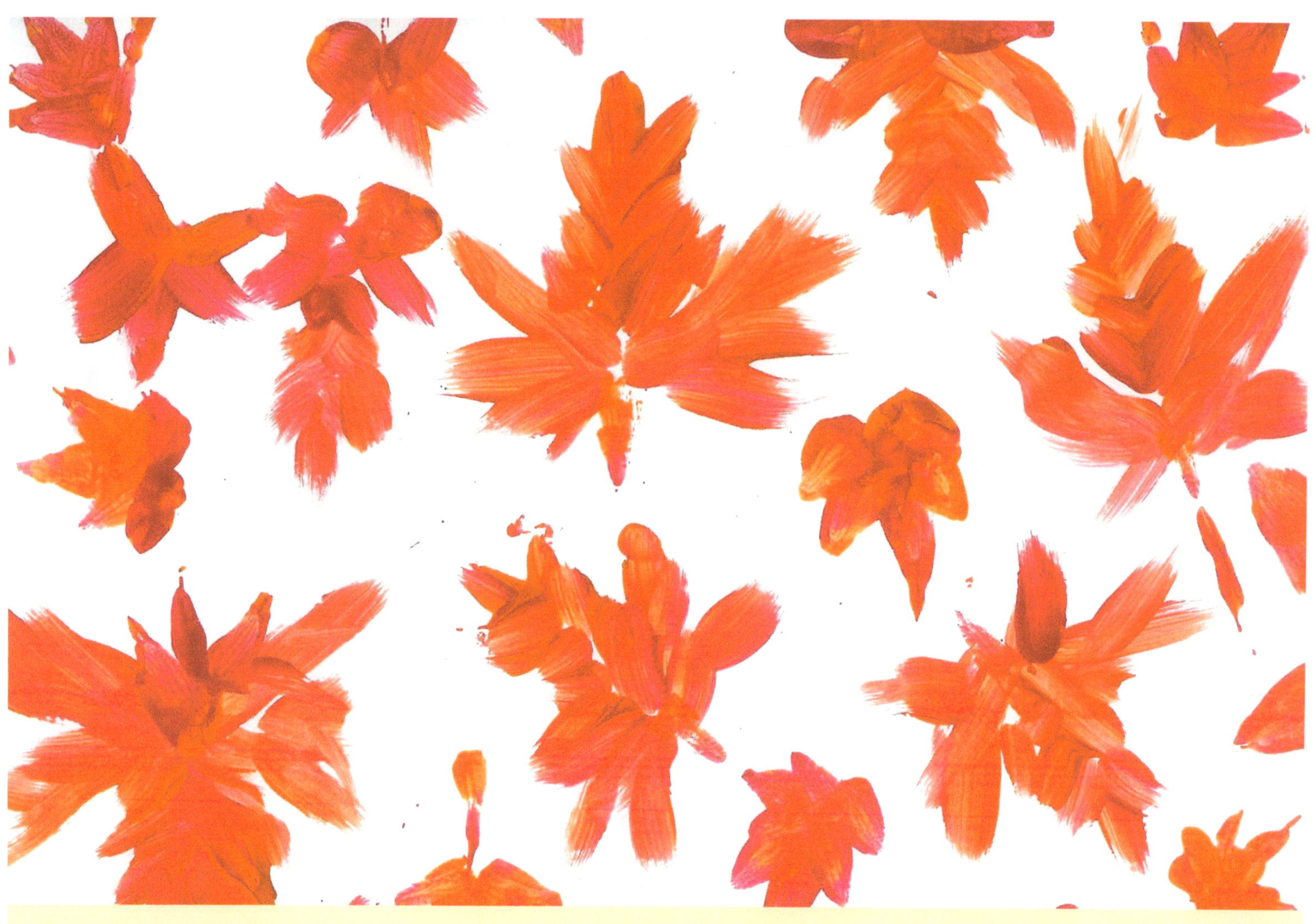

Autumn Leaves

Date completed: November 3th, 2010

On the day Candy painted this painting we took a walk around the block. During the walk Candy was stepping on the leaves and enjoying the crunching noise that they made.

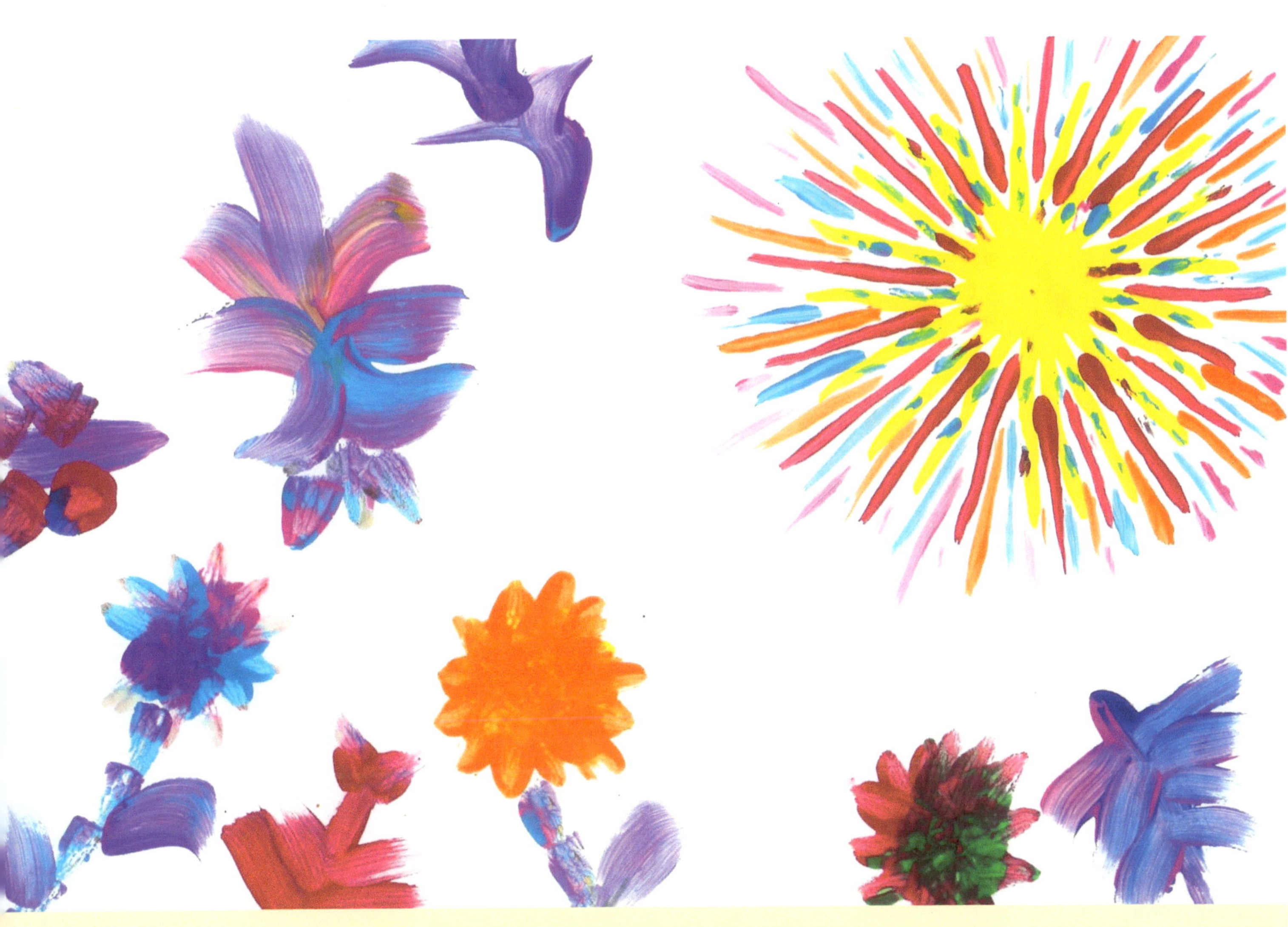

Beautiful Day

Date completed: June 29th, 2011
Candy painted this outside on a beautiful sunny day.
Candy loves the outdoors.

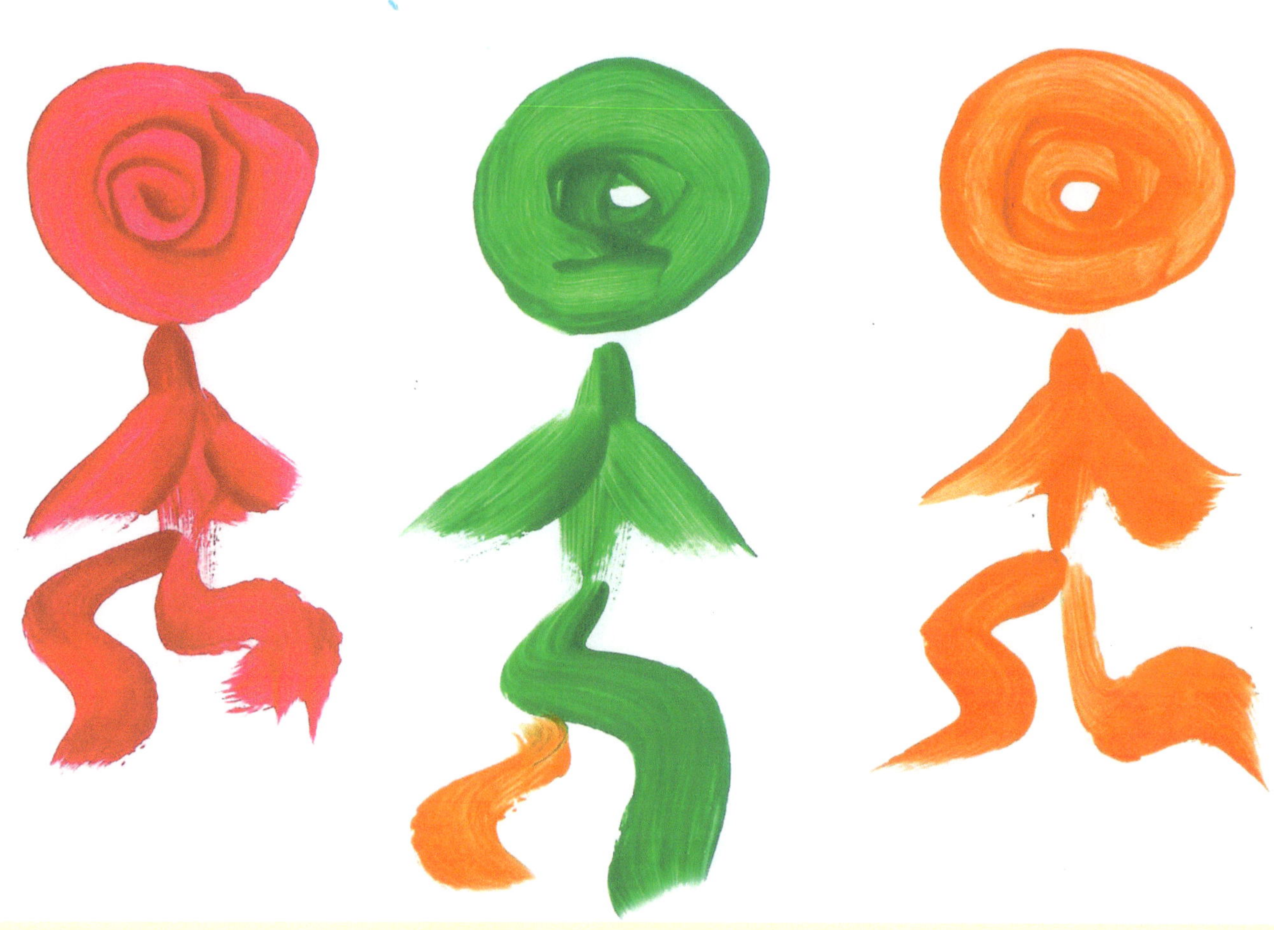

Walk Now For Autism

Date completed: April 10th, 2012

This reminded us of people walking.
This would be perfect for advertising
at Autism Awareness Walks.

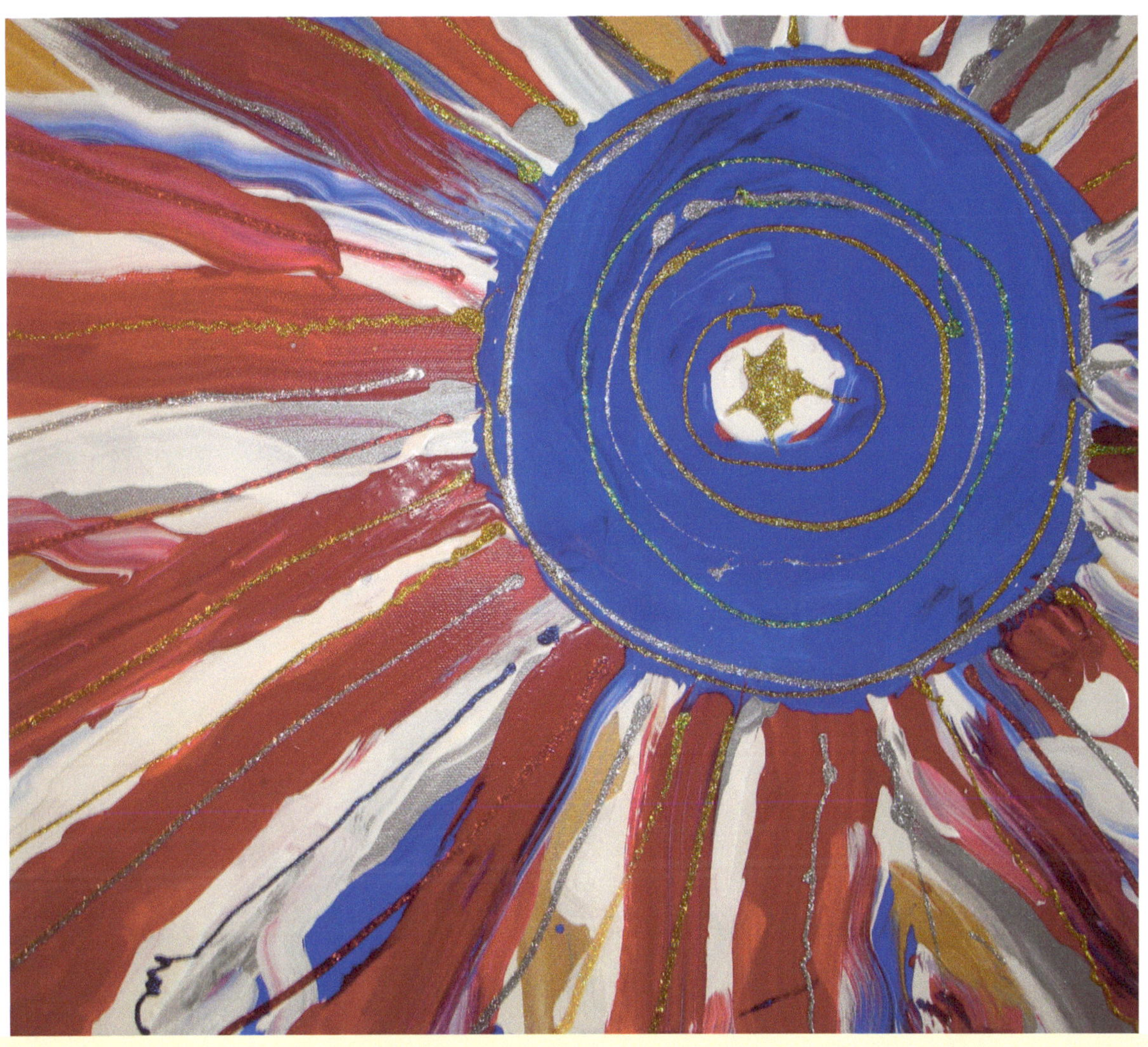

Star Spangled Sun

Date completed: July 1st, 2012

We had a flag in the yard and Candy liked
watching it wave in the wind.

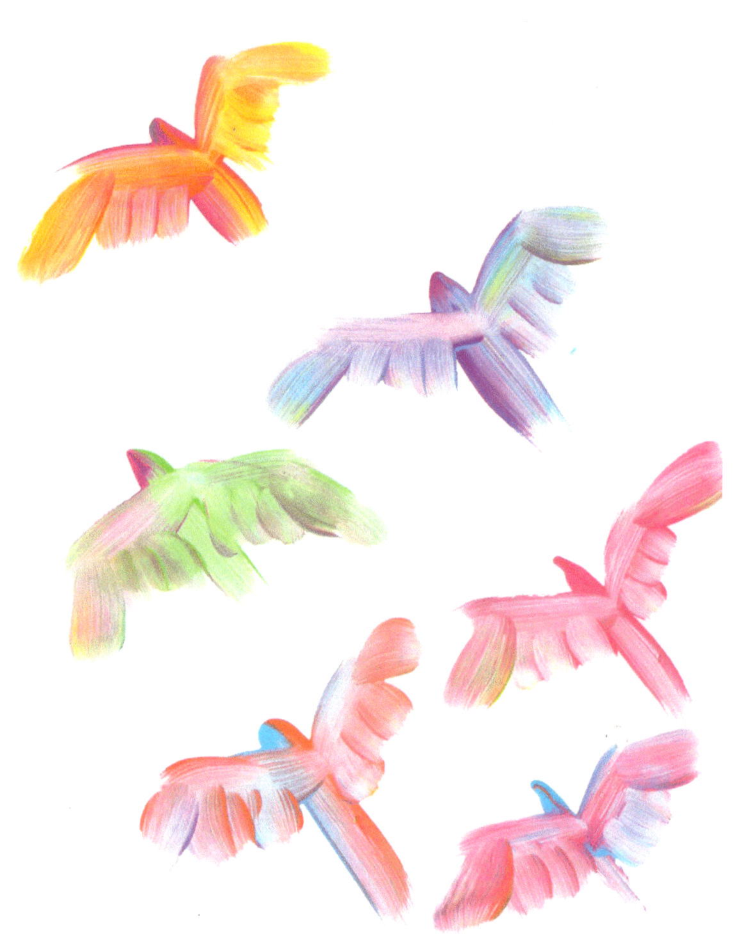

Migration

Date completed: November 27th, 2012

Candy loves watching the birds fly in formation.

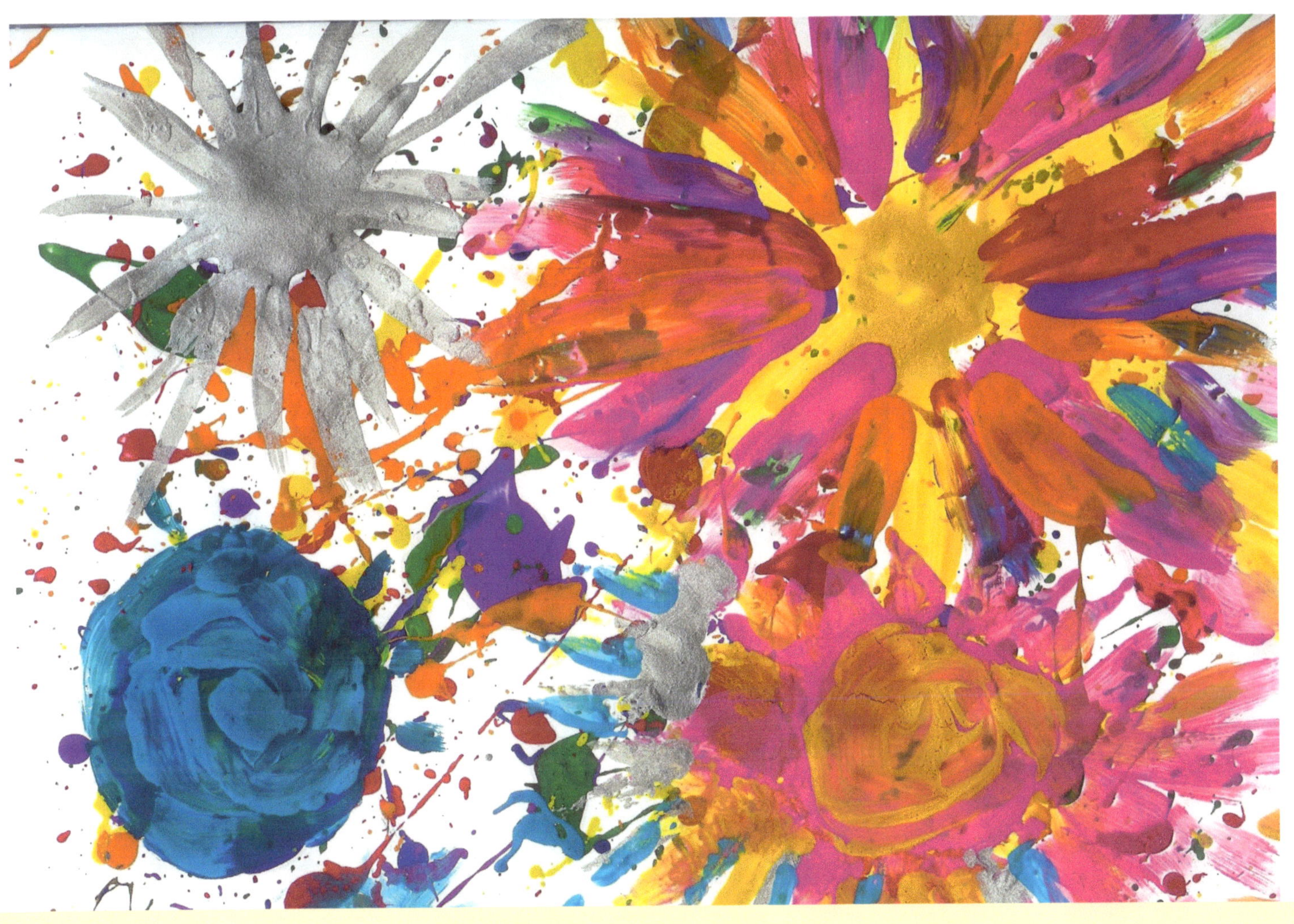

Across the Universe

Date completed: November 28th, 2012

On the night Candy painted this painting
there was an eclipse of the moon....

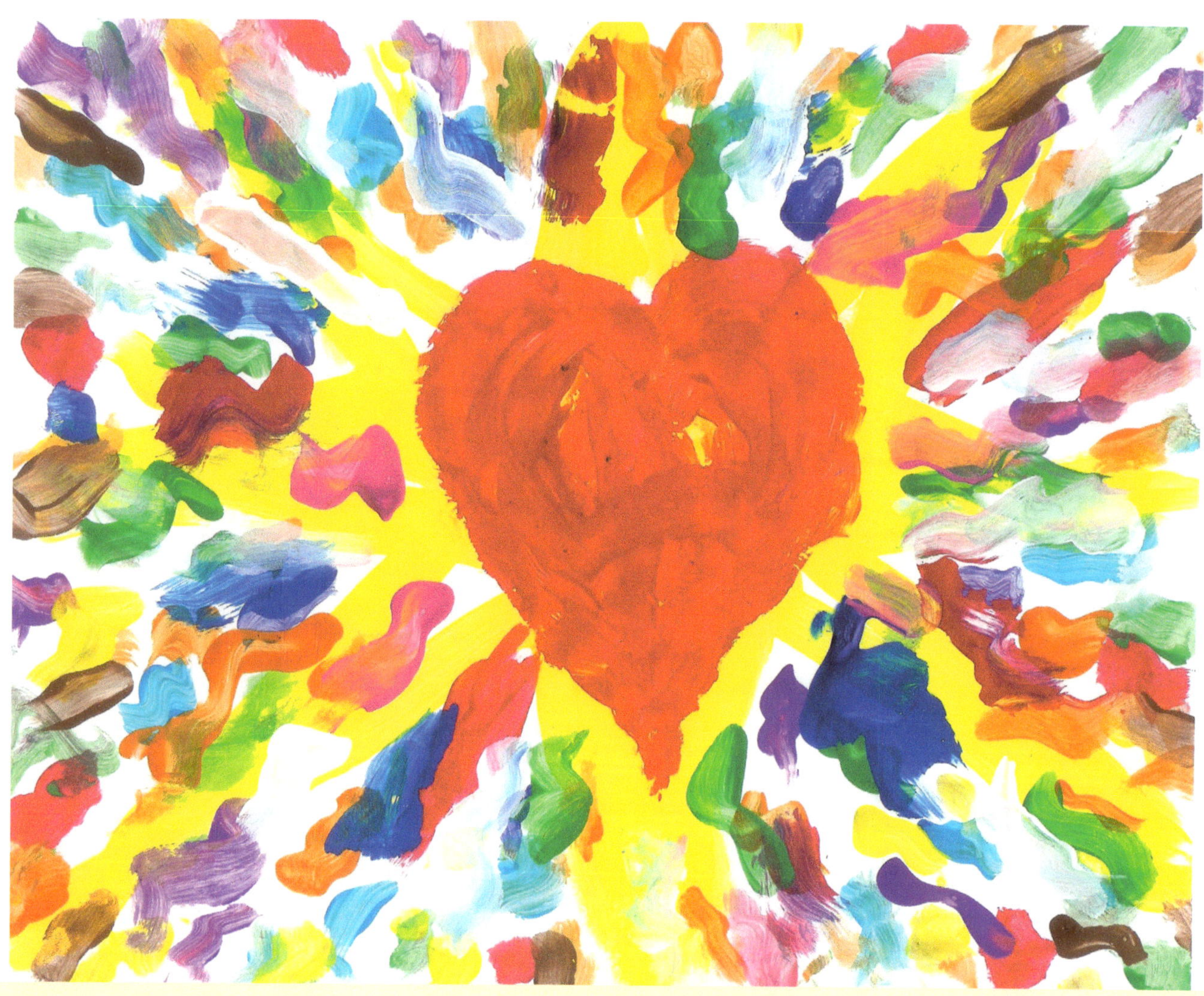

Heart Candy

Date completed: February 14th, 2013

This piece reminded us of the Sweethearts
candies for Valentines Day.

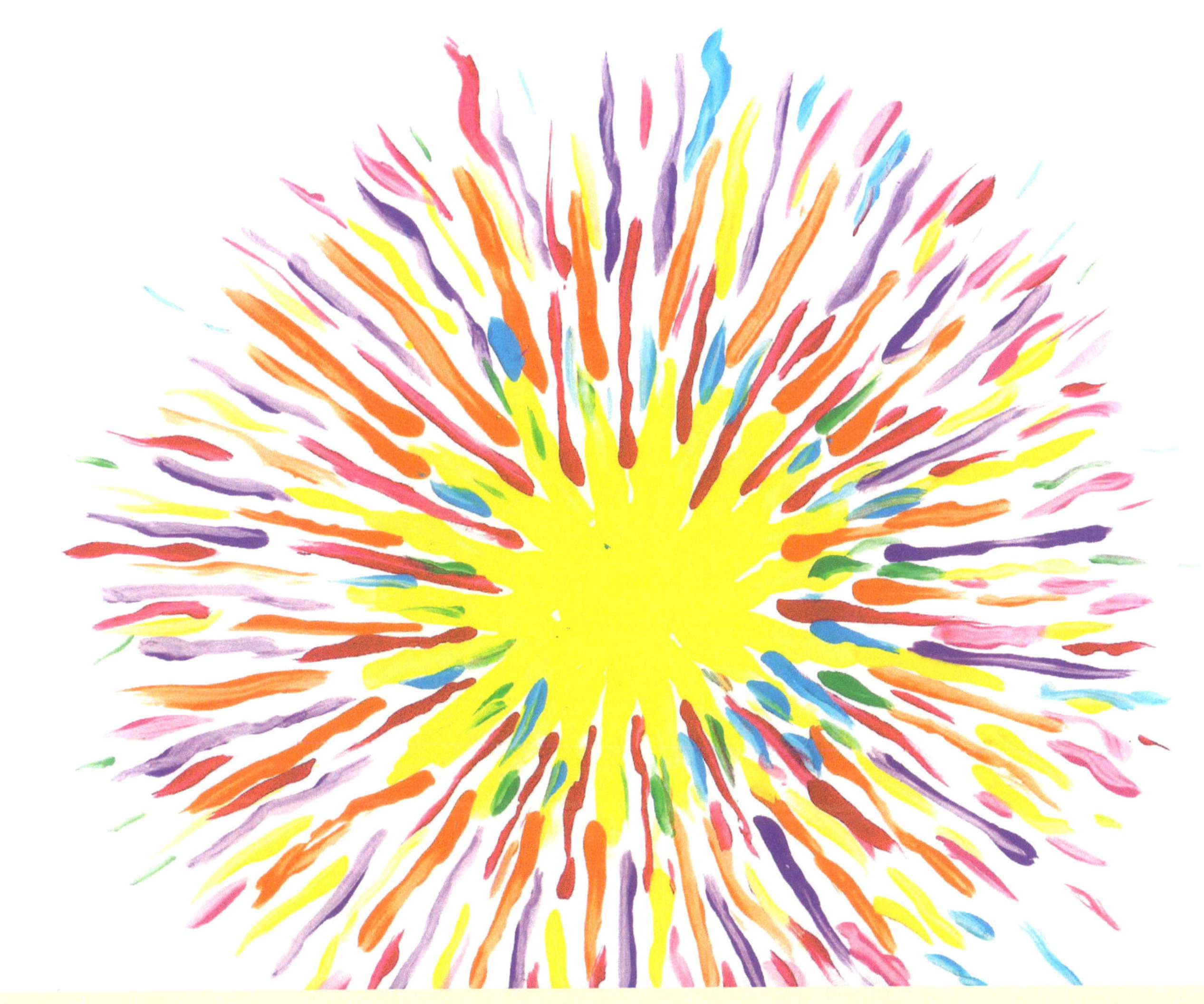

Radiance

Date completed: March 14th, 2013

This painting seems to have a pulse if you watch it long enough.

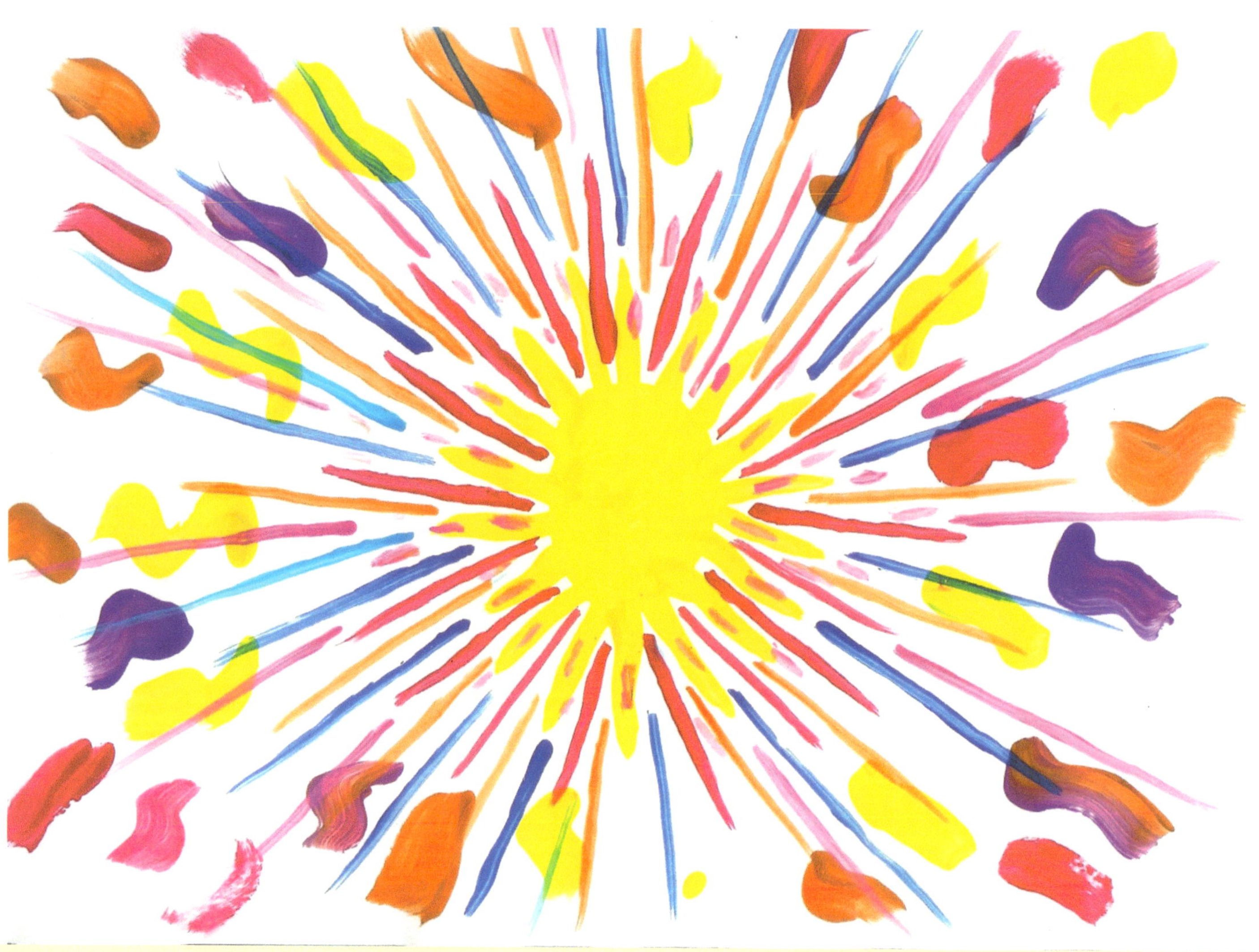

Suntastic

Date completed: May 10th, 2013

This was a new kind of sun Candy started to paint.

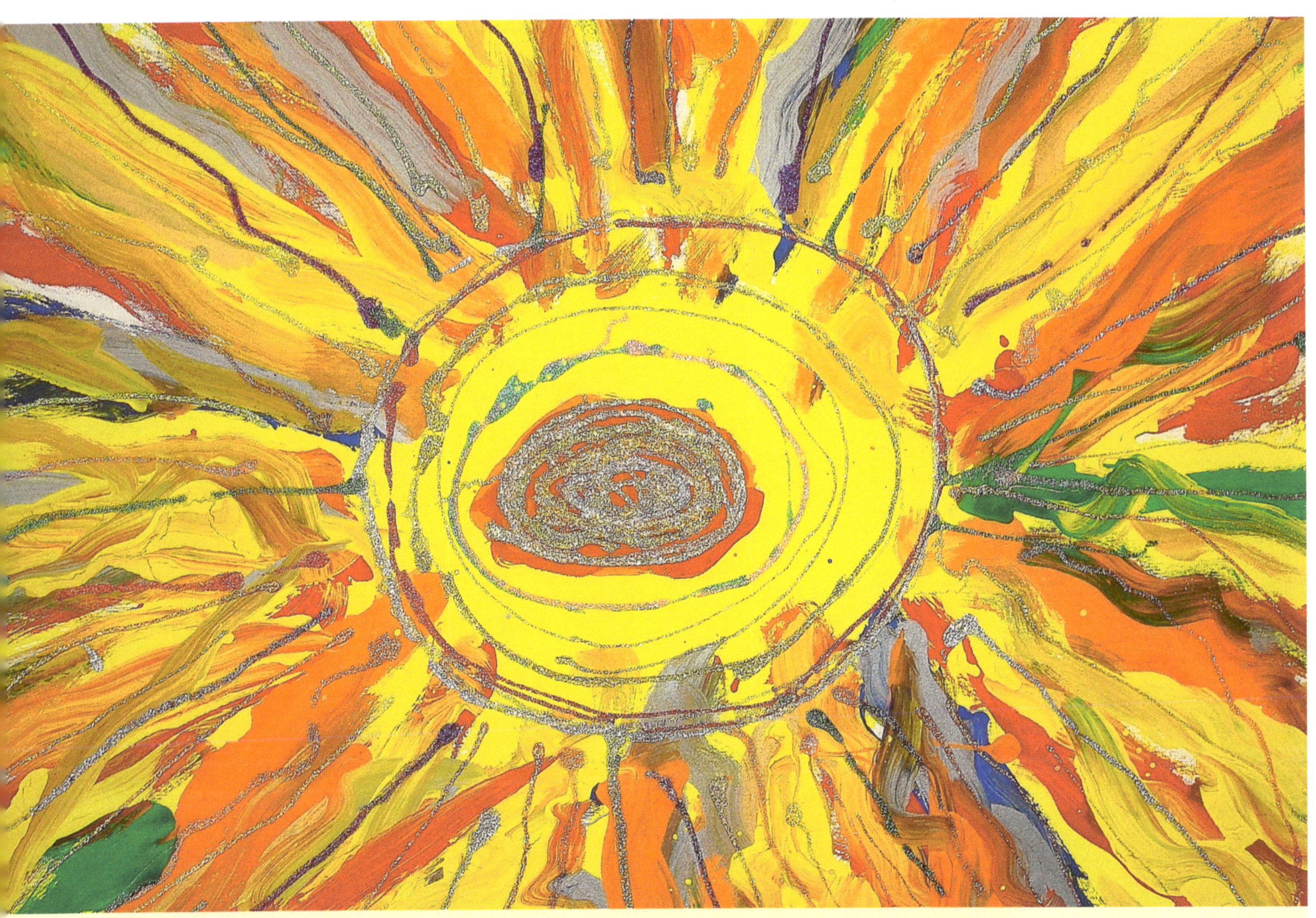

Mr. Sun

Summer 2013 Issue

On the Cover of the University of California, Irvine Magazine.
We did not know that Candy's Mr. Sun painting was used on the
cover of UCI magazine until it came out. Great surprise!!

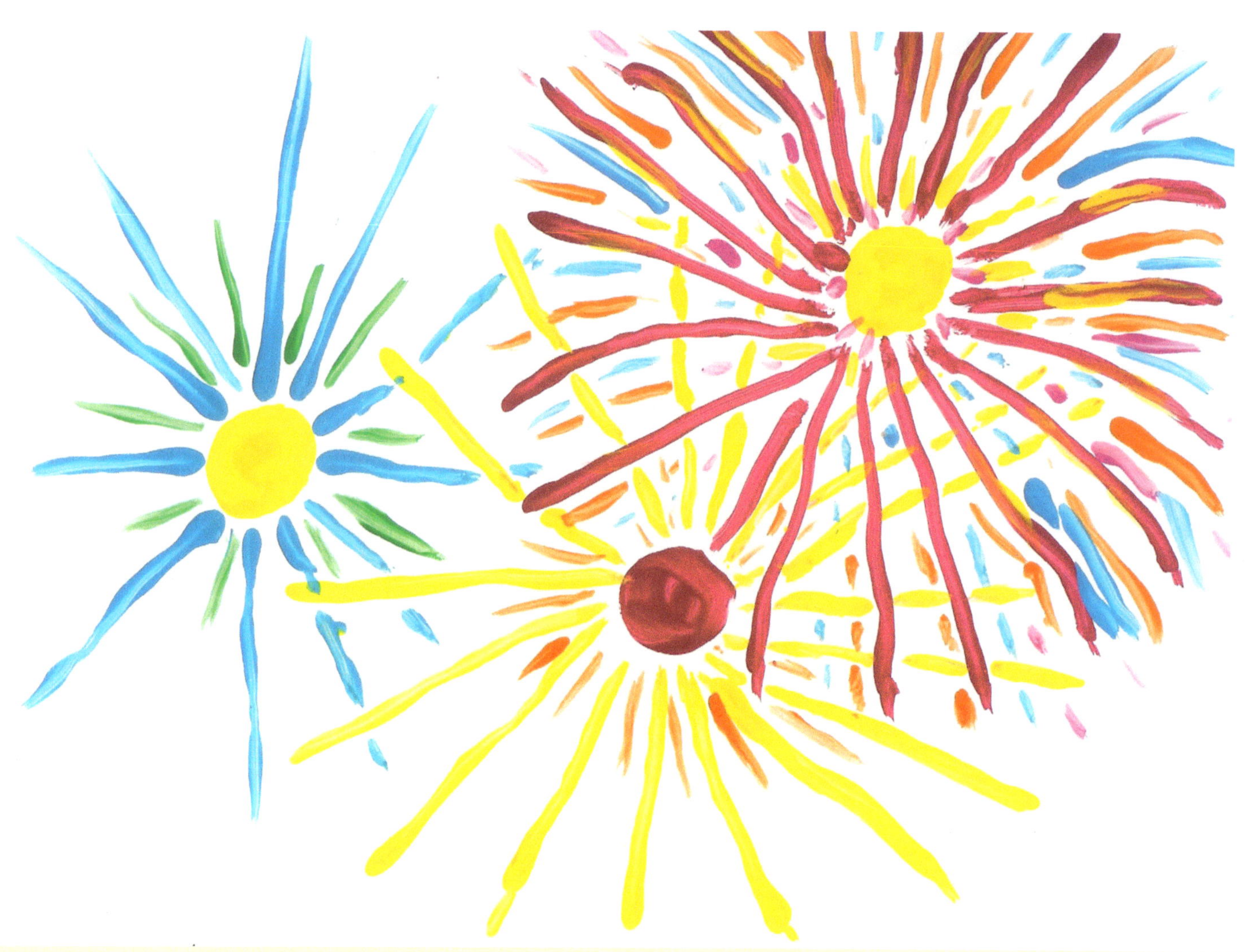

Firework

Date completed: July 4th, 2013

Candy just watched the firework display she loved it

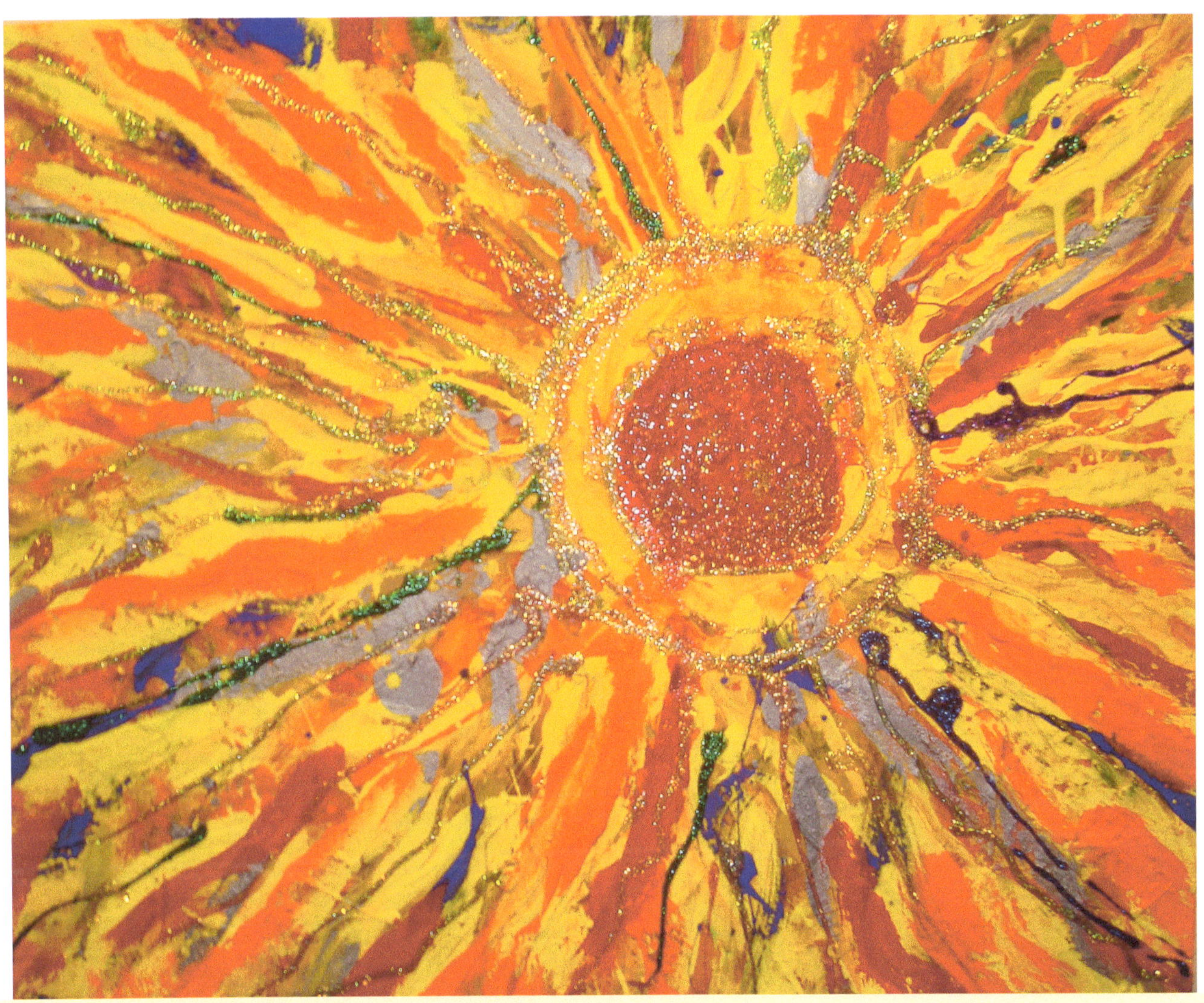

Ray of Hope

Date completed: July 14th, 2013

Football Great Dan Marino loved this painting.
This painting is displayed at the Marino Campus
in Fort Lauderdale, Florida.

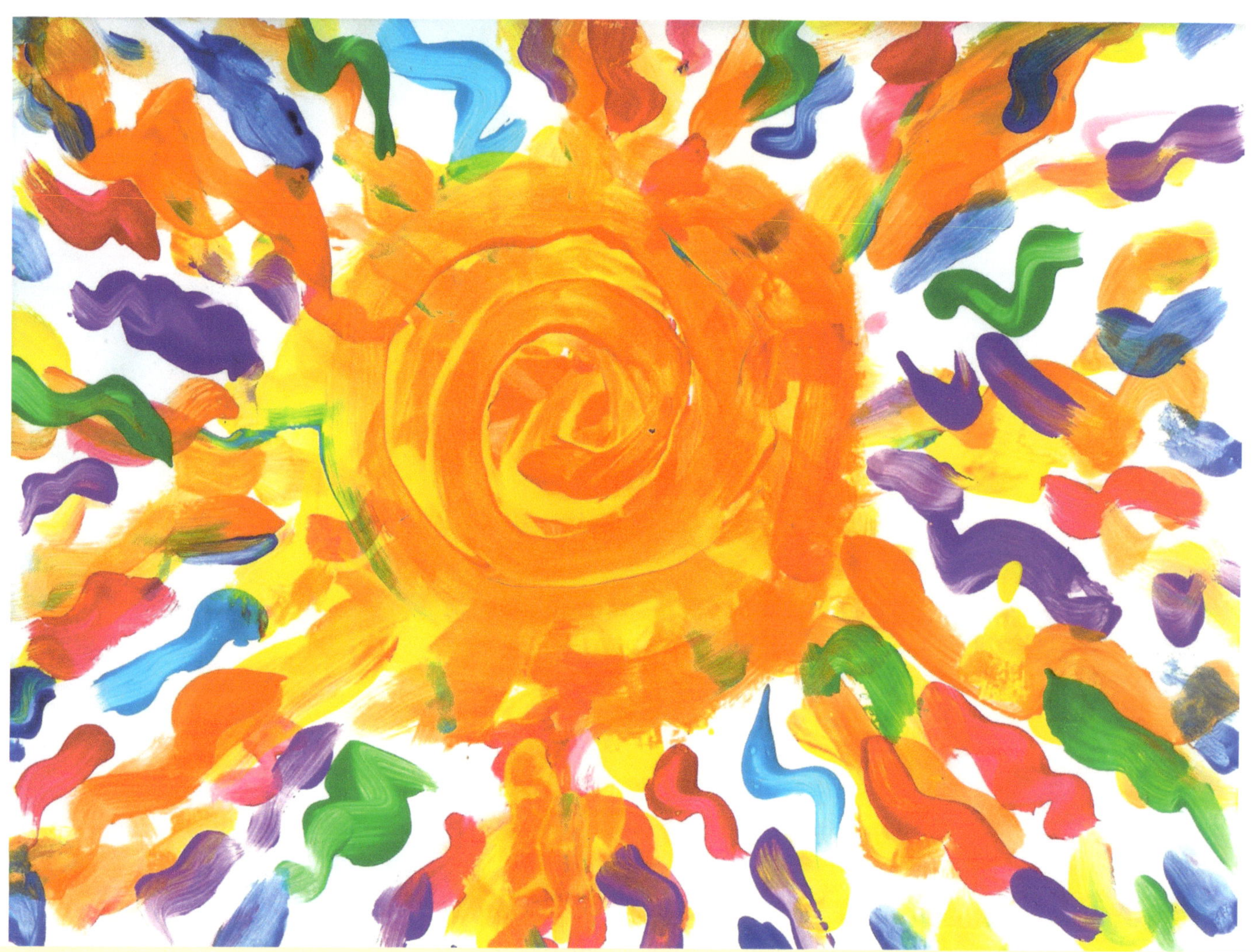

Sunfetti

Date completed: October 24th, 2013

Candy was missing the sun in October so she painted her own.

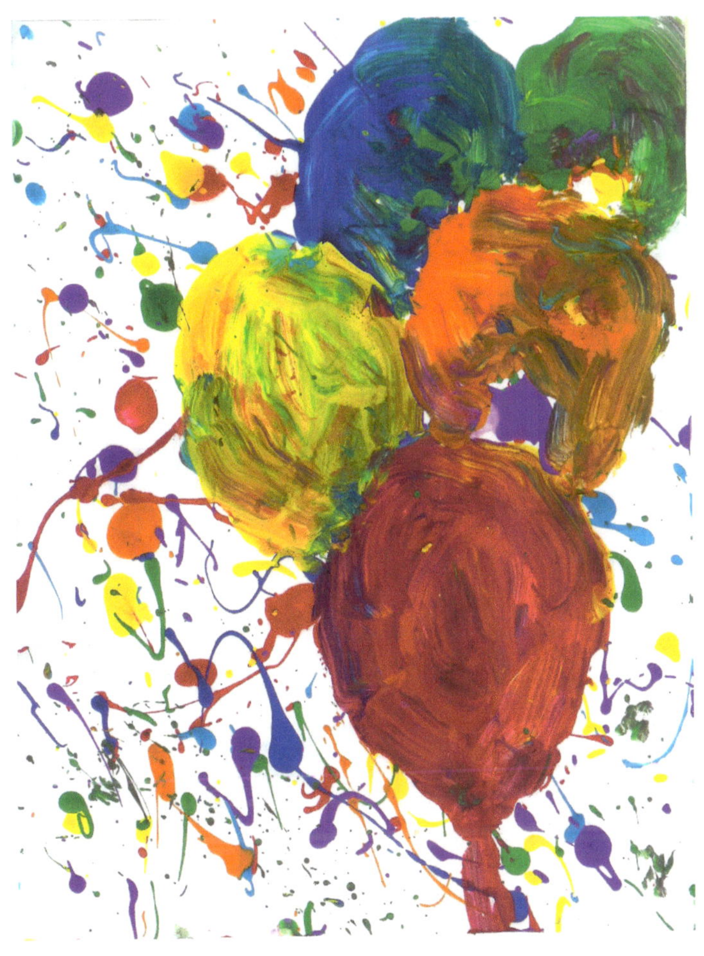

Balloonderful

Date completed: October 31st, 2013

Candy painted this painting after our son Evan's 8th birthday party.

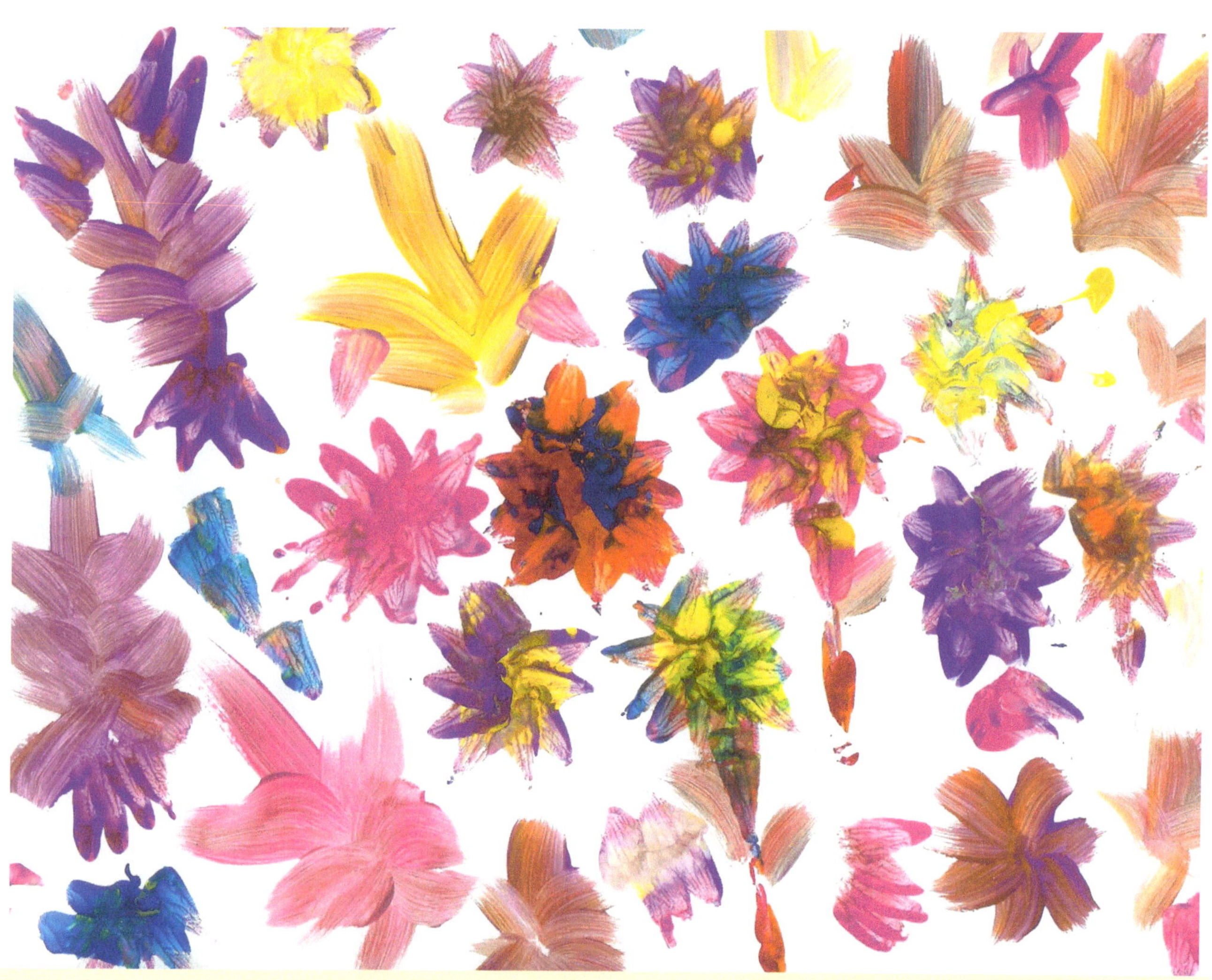

Bouquet

Date completed: November 9th, 2013

Candy has always loved flowers and smelling them.

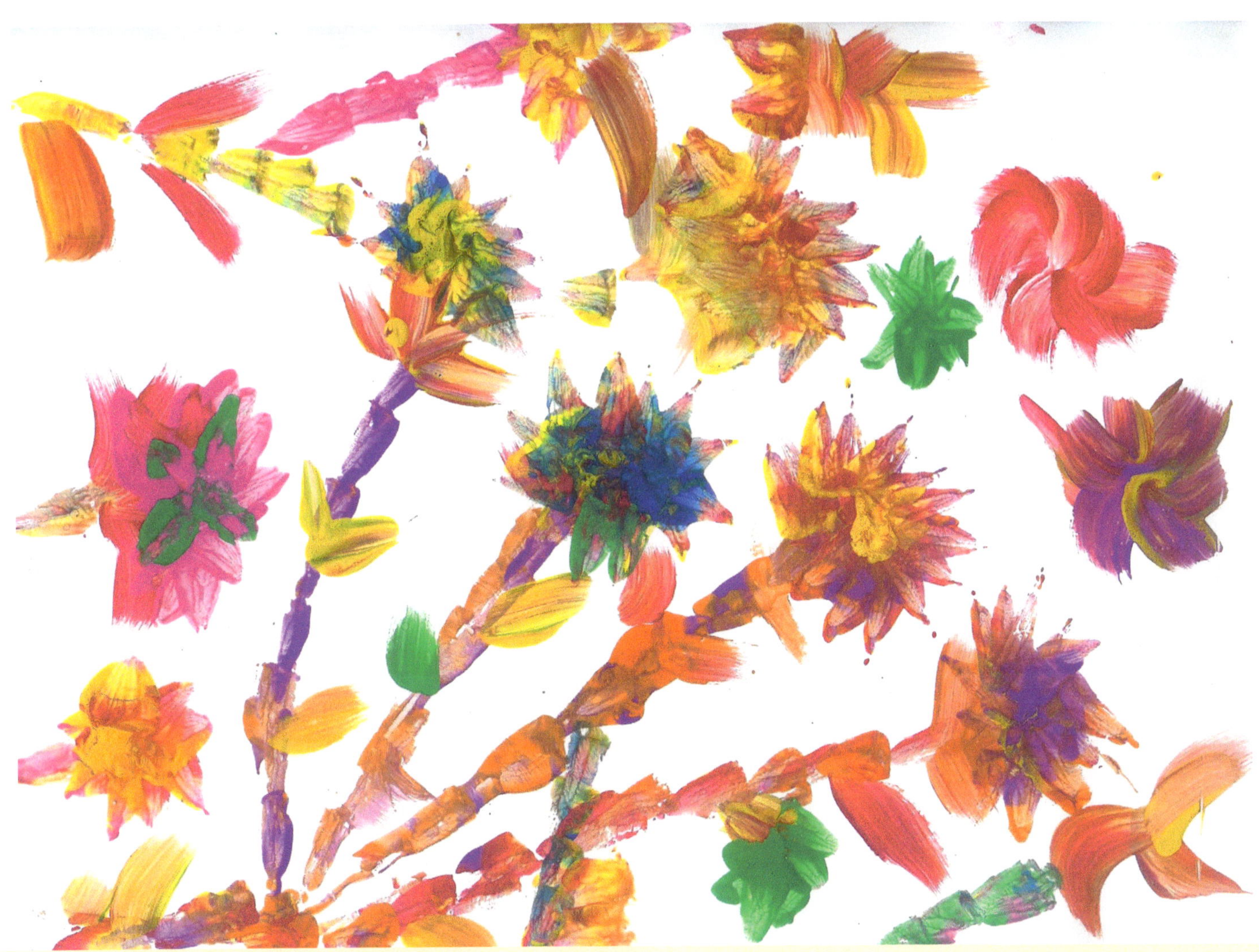

Cellophane Flowers

Date completed: November 15th, 2013

We had the Beatles album Sgt. Pepper on when Candy painted this and it reminded us of the Beatles song lyric Cellophane Flowers.

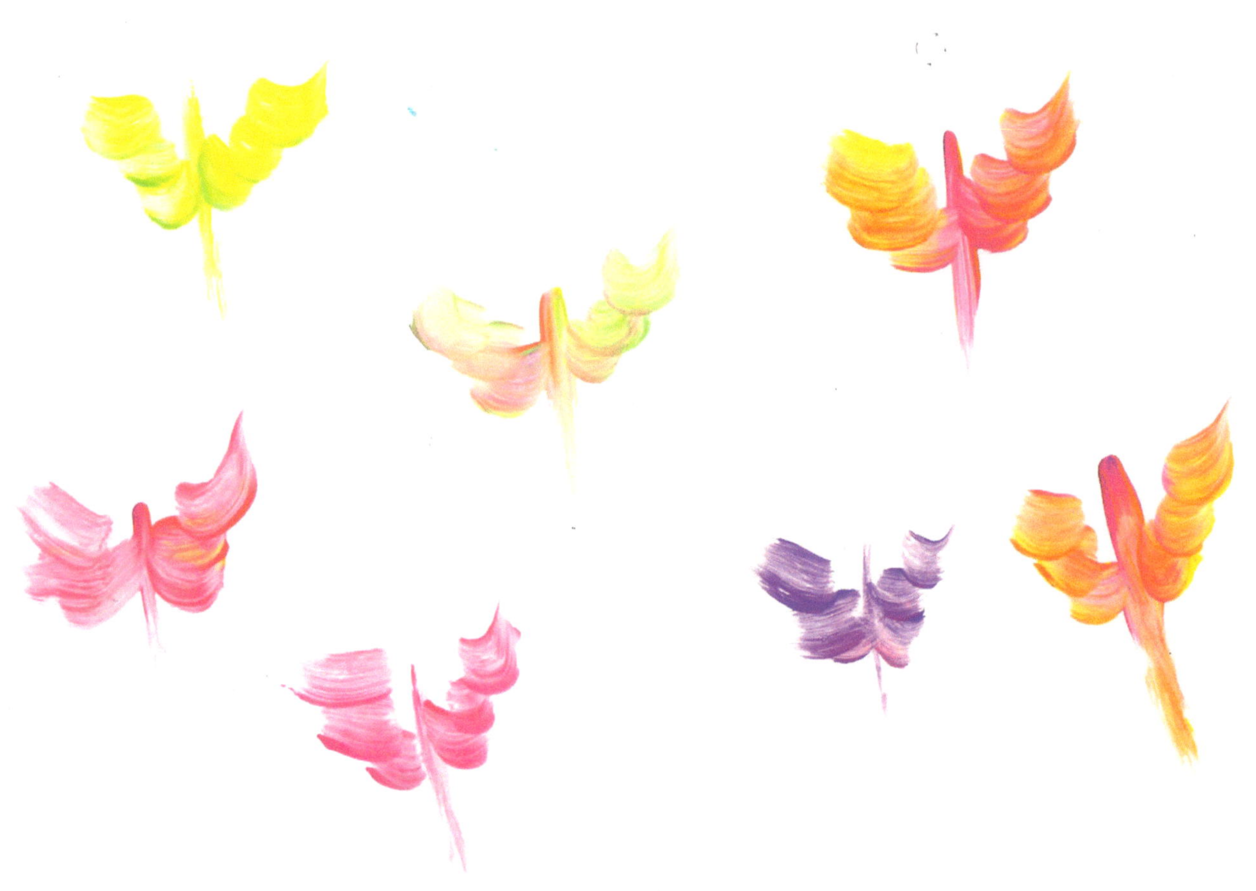

Flight

Candy was looking up in the air periodically when she painted this painting. It's as if she sees these flying around her and they are modeling for Candy. We like to think so.

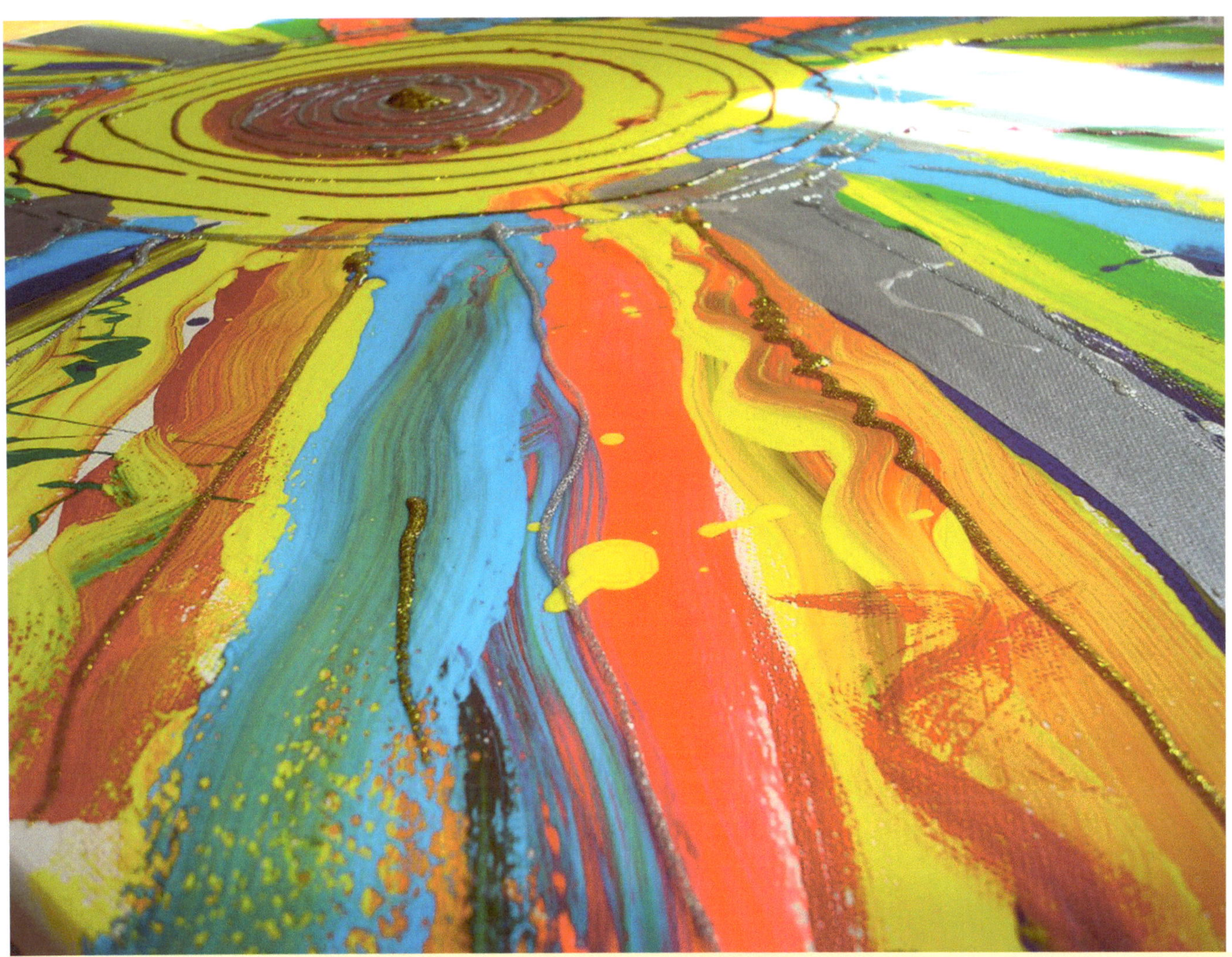

Candy Speaks

Date completed: April 15th, 2014

This painting is displayed in the Autism Speaks Chicago office. Candy painted this painting and we donated it to the Autism Speaks Chicago Office.

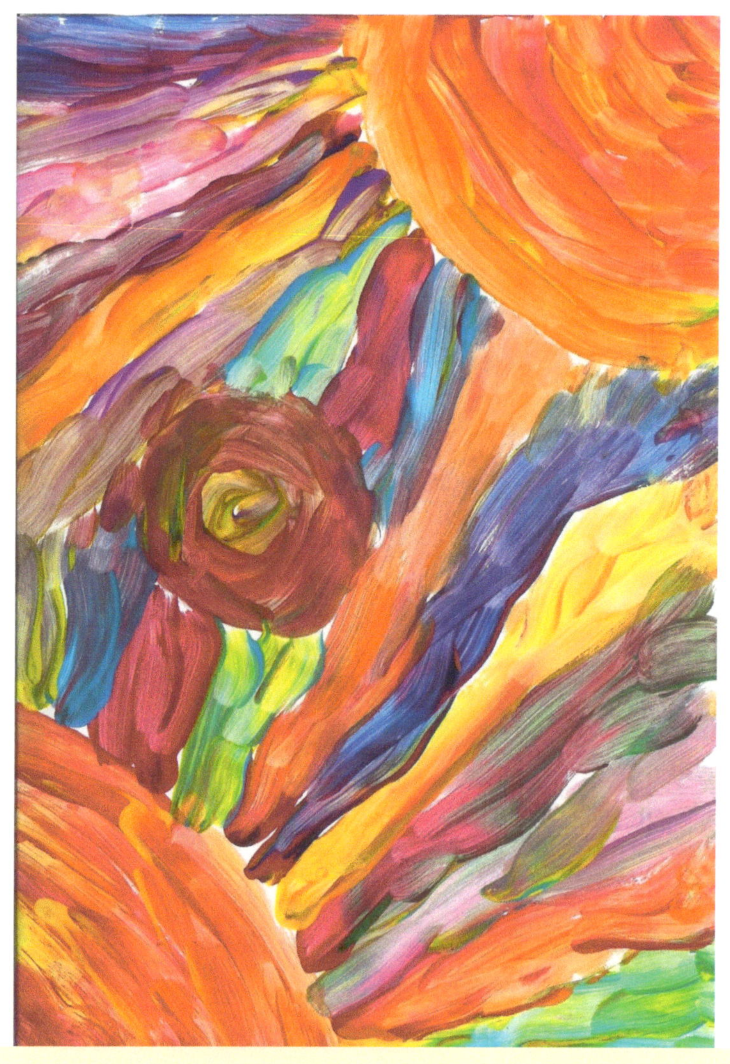

Between Two Worlds

Date completed: May 24th, 2014
Candy seemed more serious when she painted this
painting. Some people tell us that they see an
eye in the middle circle. We do see the eye.
We wish we knew what it means.

Soaring

Candy seemed so free when she painted this painting. We feel if she could fly she would.

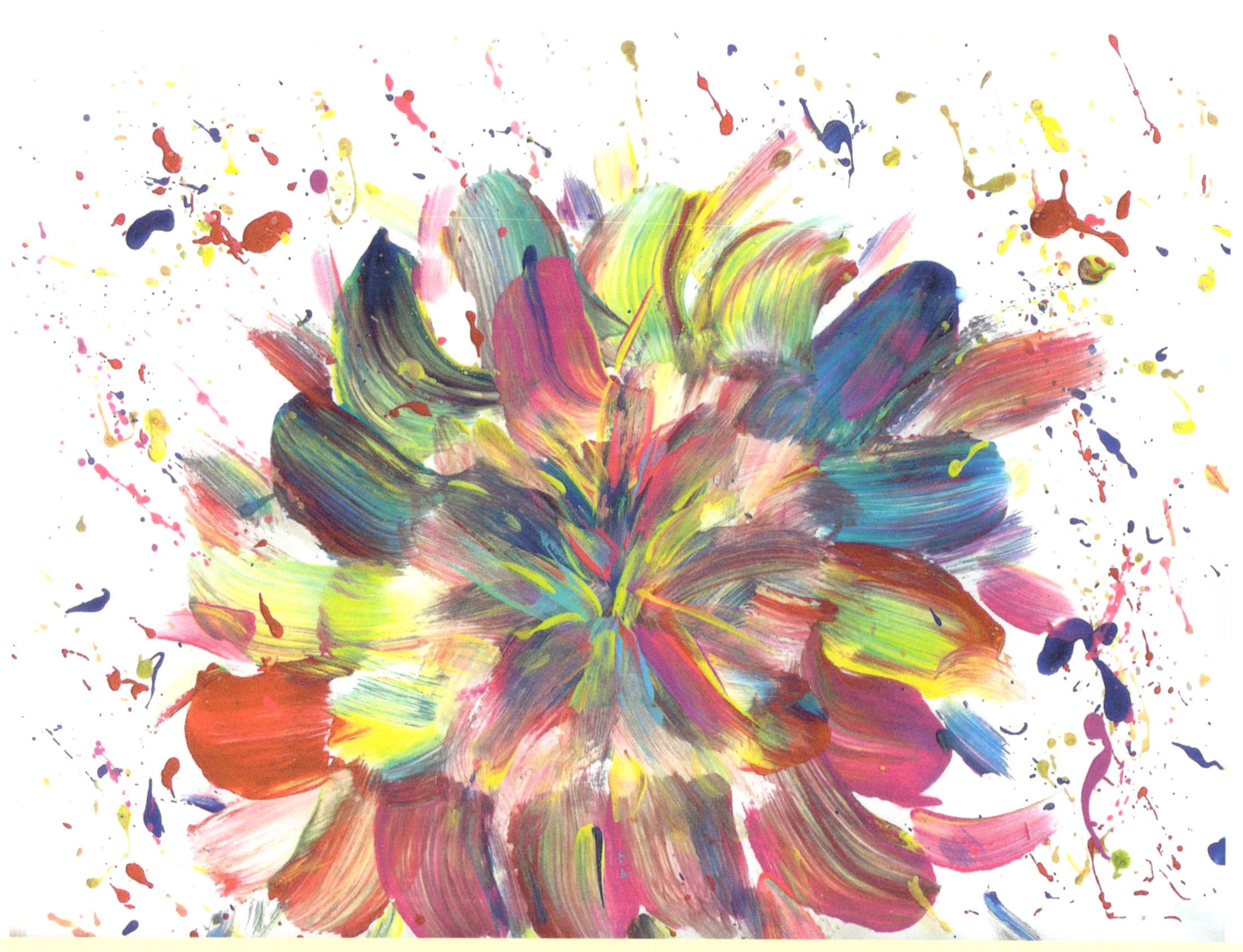

Eruption

Date completed: May 29th, 2014

Candy had a great time painting this piece.

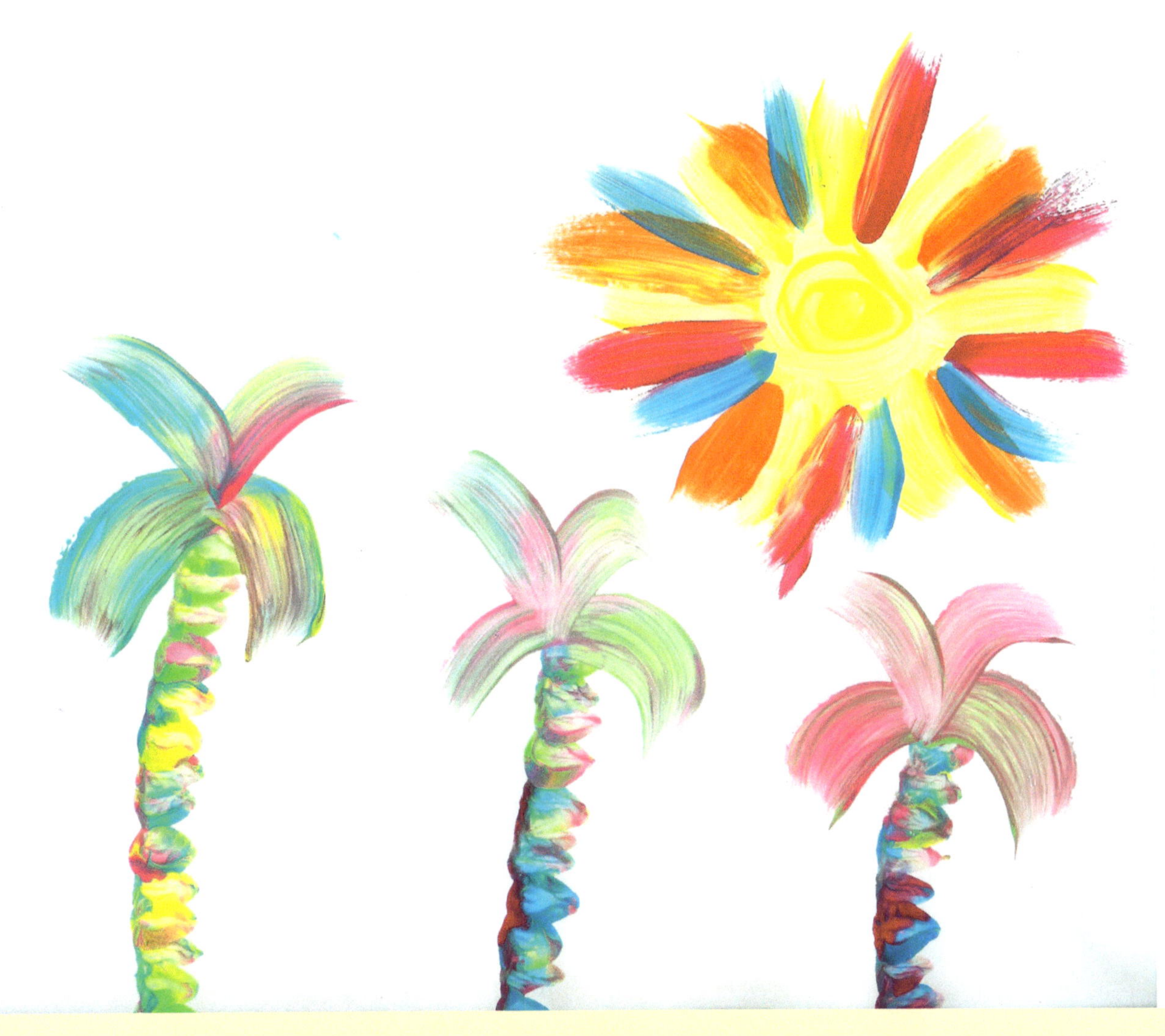

Palm Trees & Paradise

Date completed: June 23rd, 2014
Candy loved blending the colors for this painting.

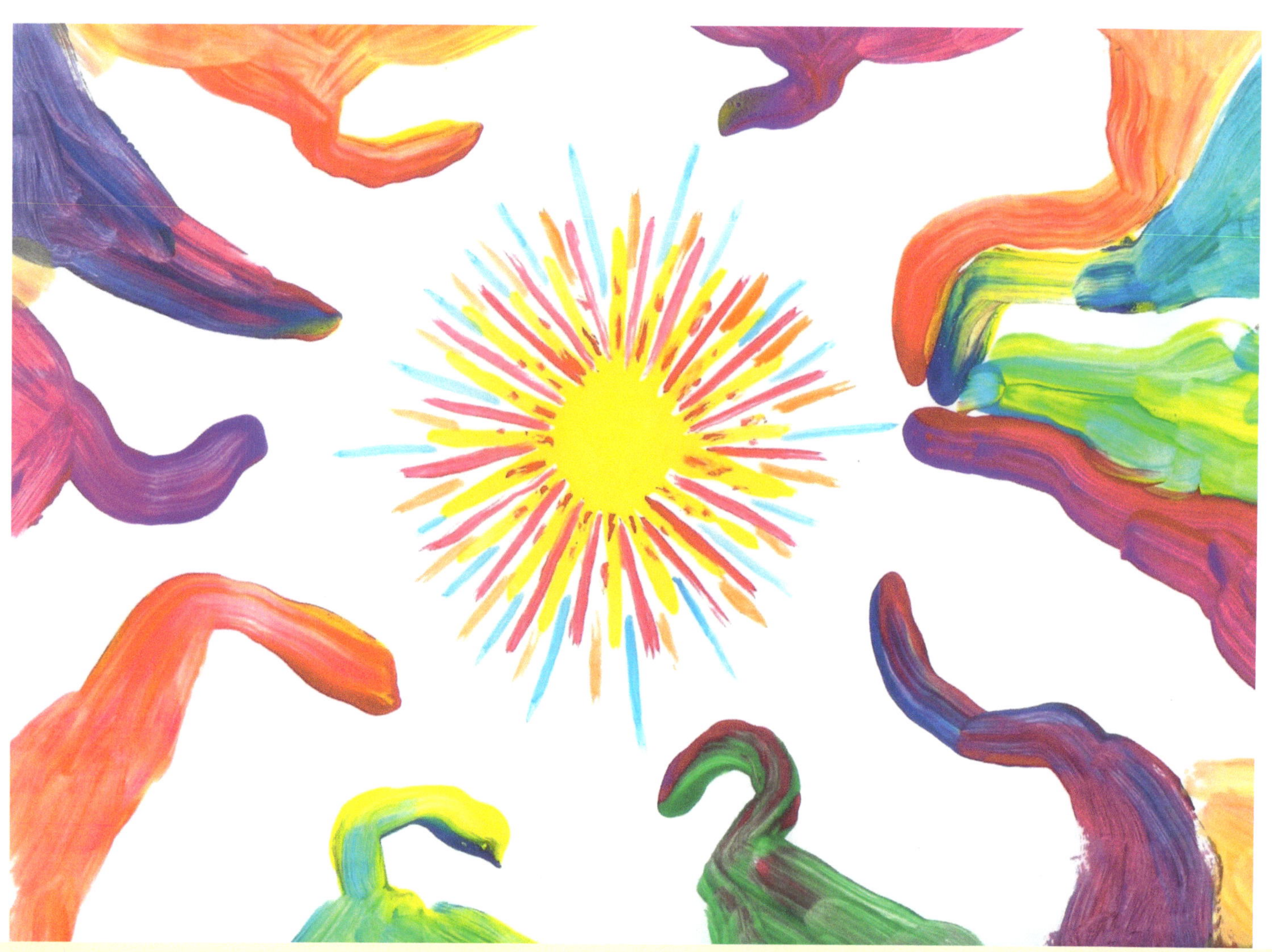

Mountain Tops

Date completed: September 1st, 2014

This feels like you are looking up at mountain tops.

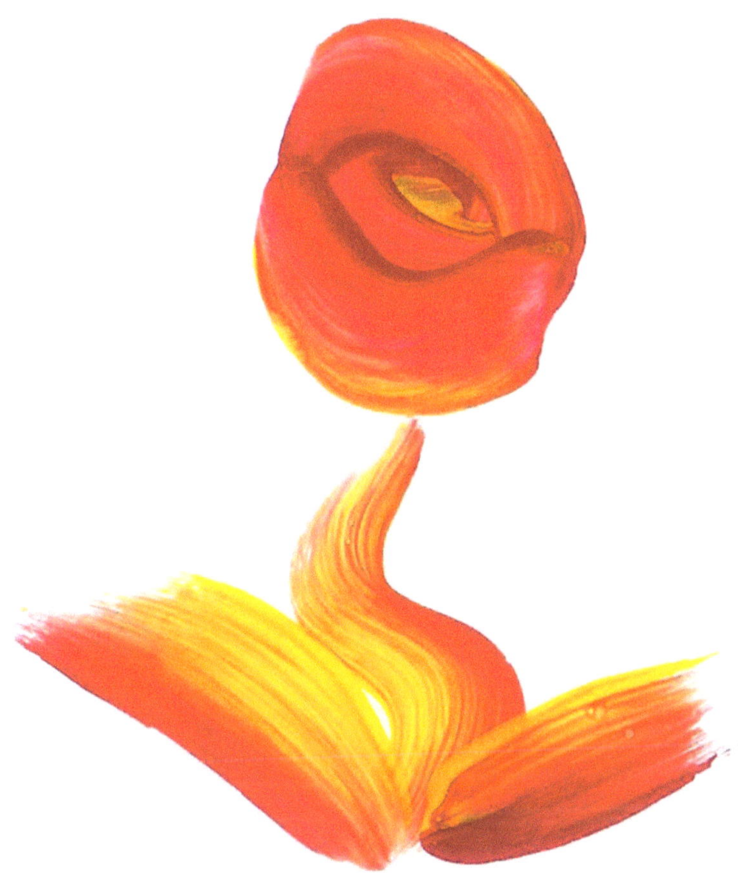

Flower Candy

Date completed: September 27th, 2014

Candy painted this painting on her Grandmother's Birthday.

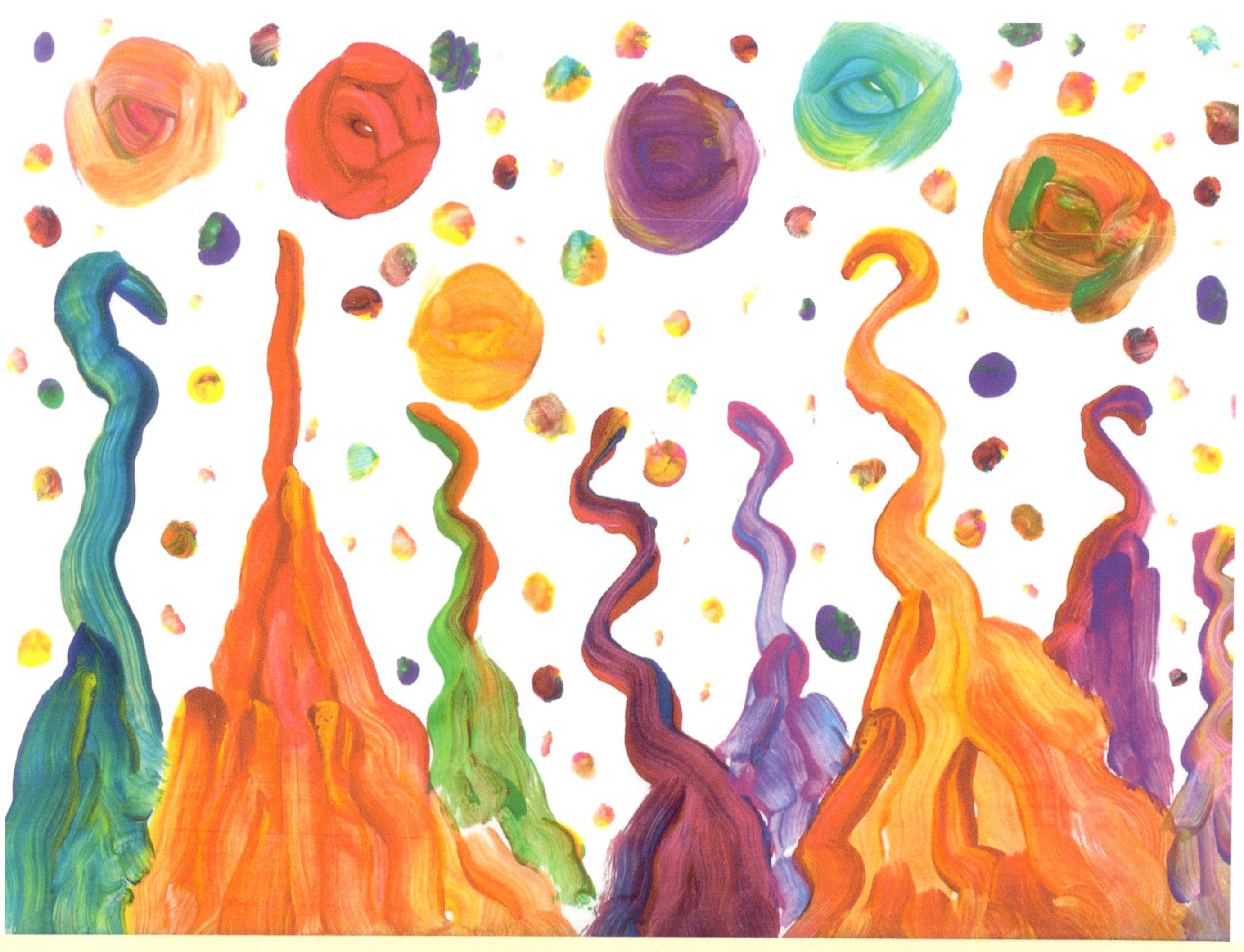

Candyland

Date completed: September 15th, 2014

Candy just started to paint these curvy color lines.

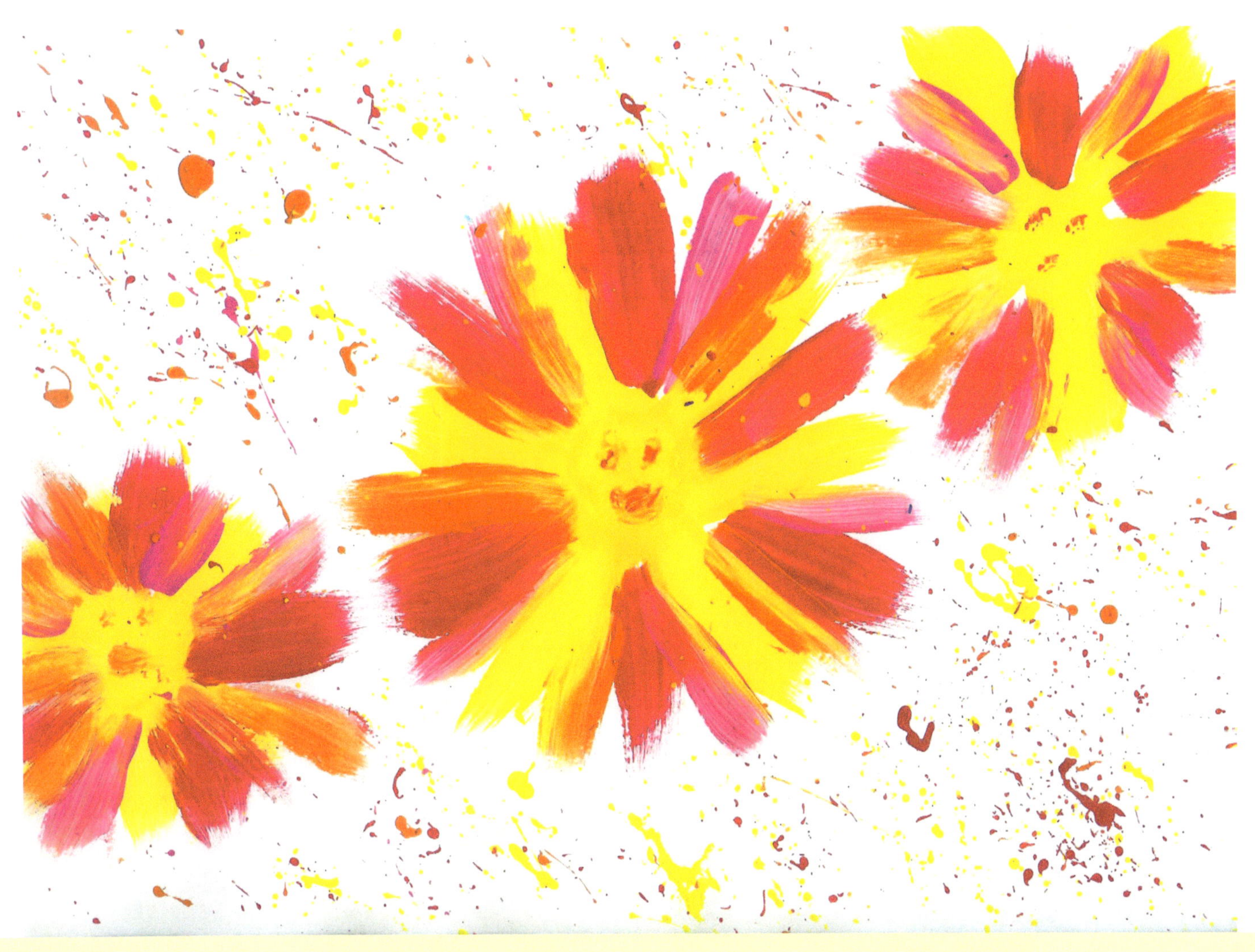

My 3 Suns

Date completed: March 10th, 2015

This is the first time I have seen faces in Candy's art.

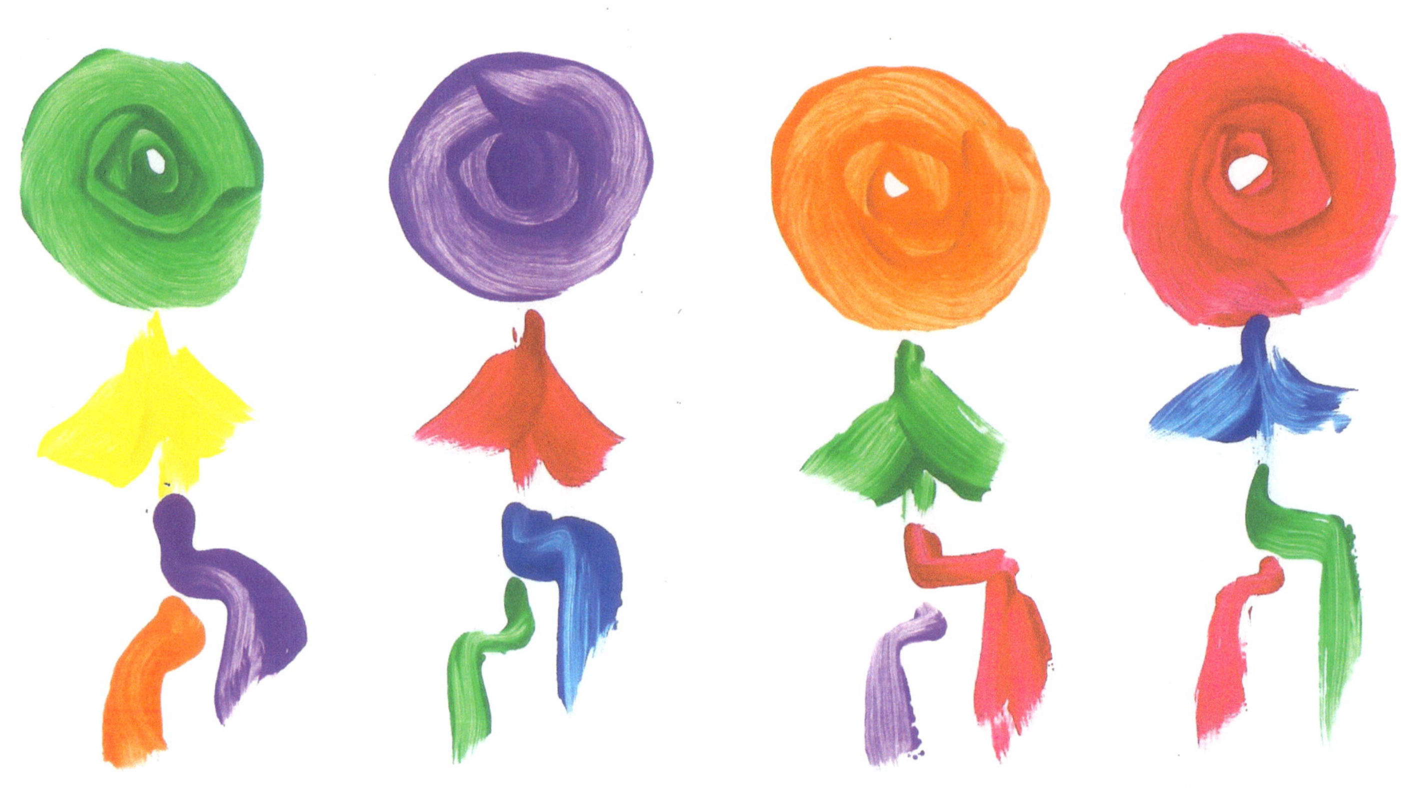

Abbey Road

Date completed: May 14th, 2015

Candy loves to listen to Beatles music when she paints. We had Abbey Road on when Candy painted this painting and we put the album cover in front of Candy and this was the end result.

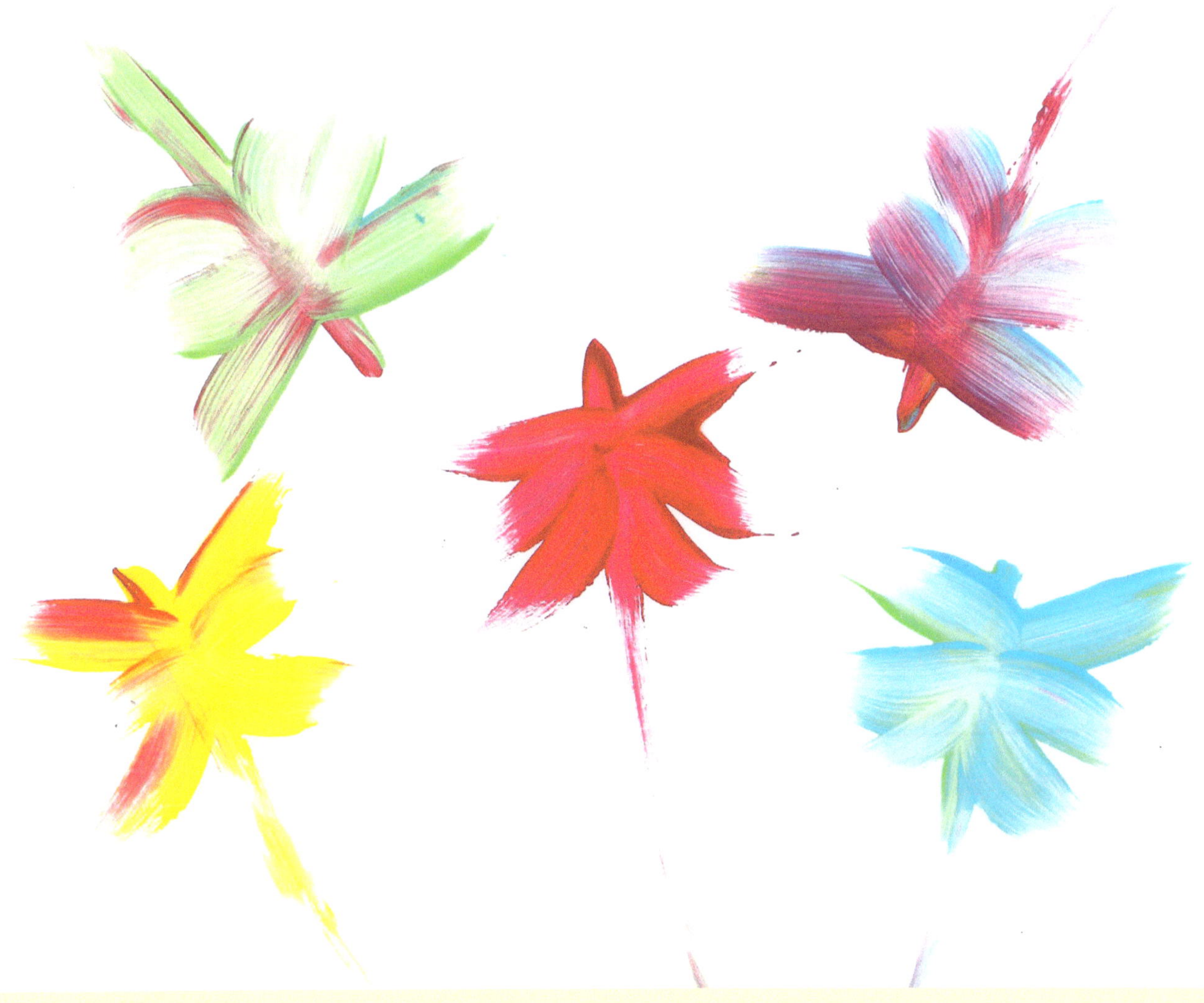

Dragonflies

Date completed: May 30th, 2015

Candy has always been fascinated with anything that flies

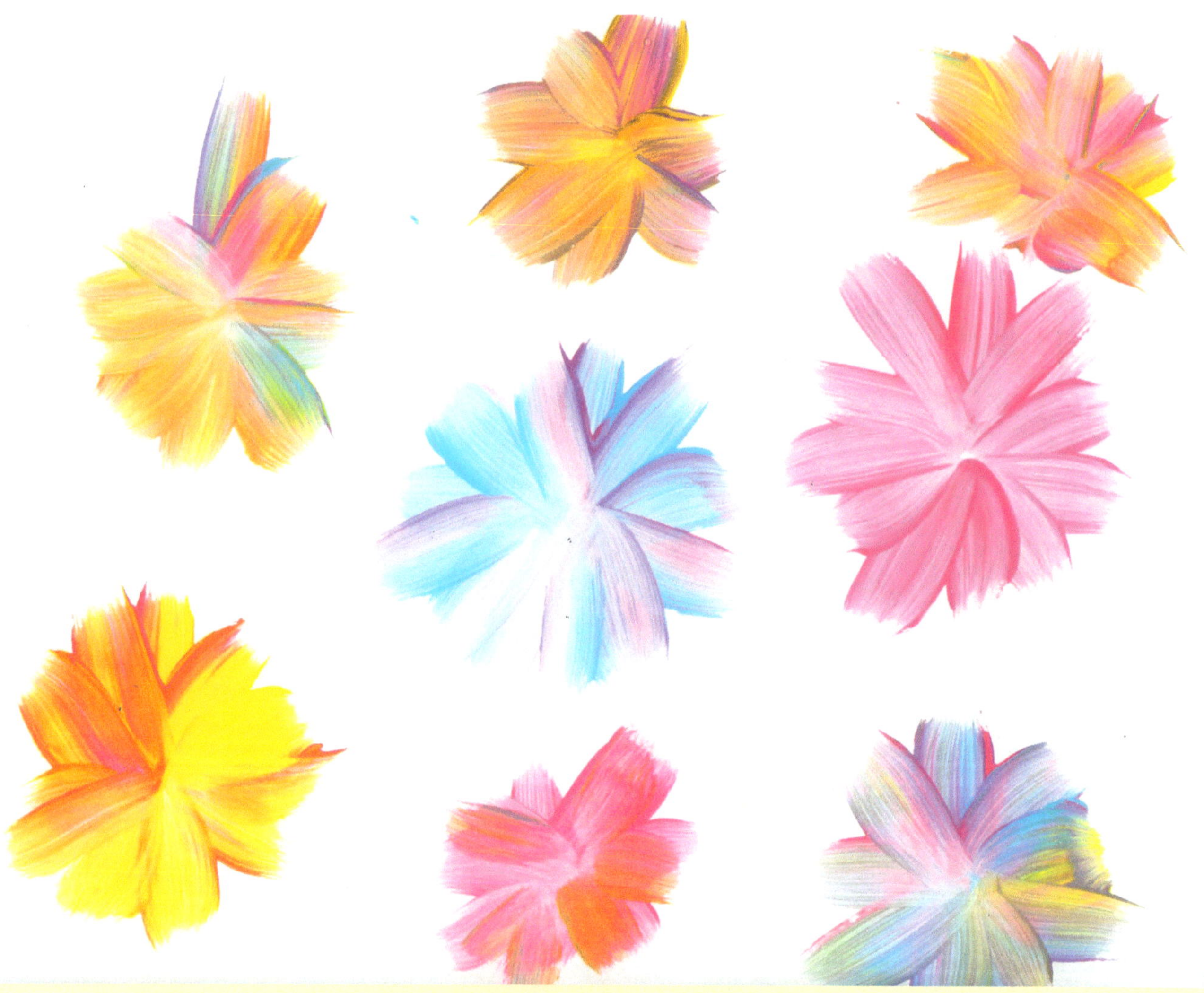

Snowflakes

Date completed: May 31st, 2015

Candy loves to blend colors together it is her trademark.

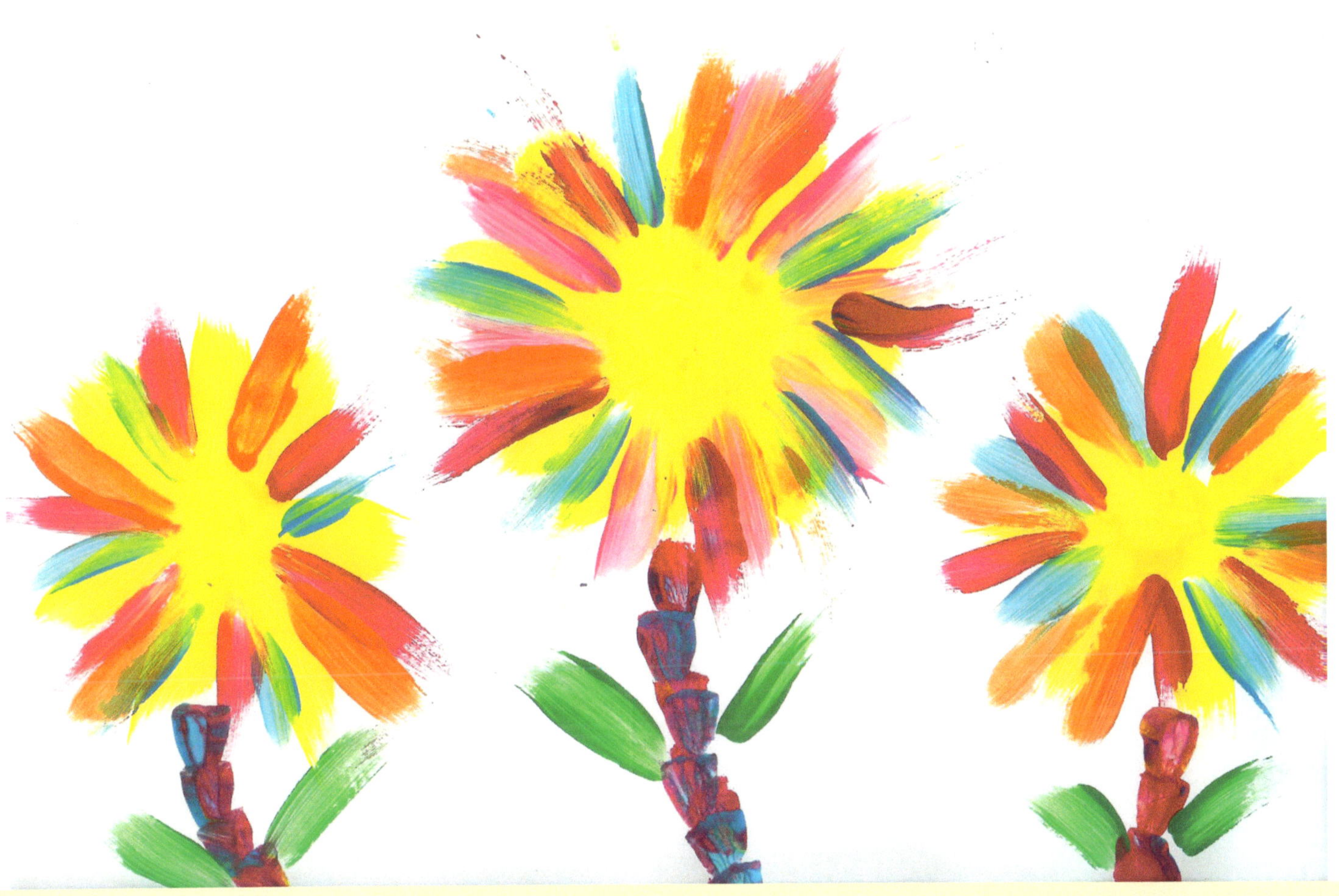

Flower Power

Candy loves painting flowers and suns. This piece seems to be a mix of a little bit of both.

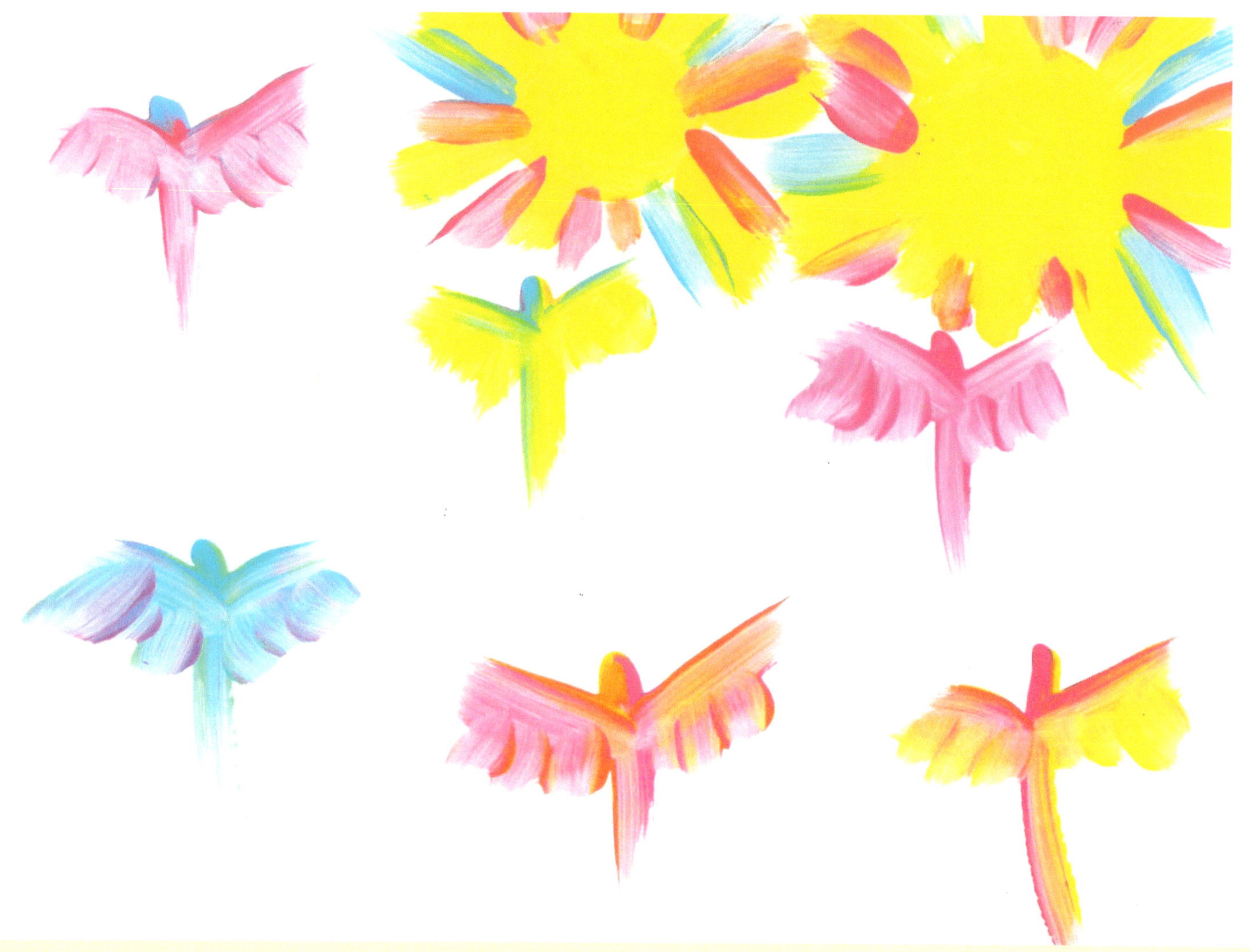

Ascension

Date completed: June 13th, 2015

Candy was very happy and kept looking up in the air
when she painted this. We think Candy sees these.

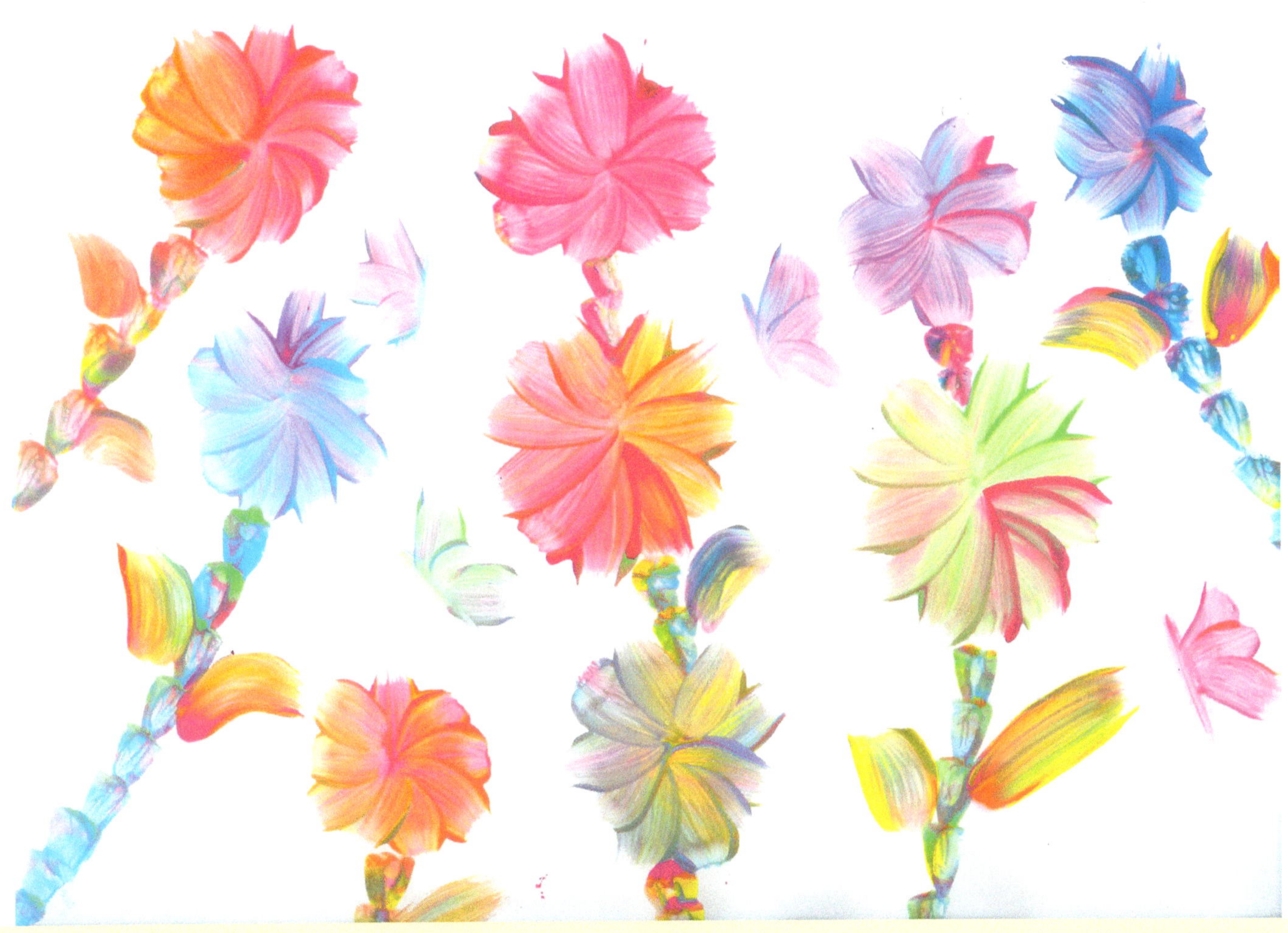

Dancing

Date completed: June 30th, 2015
Candy loves colorful flowers.

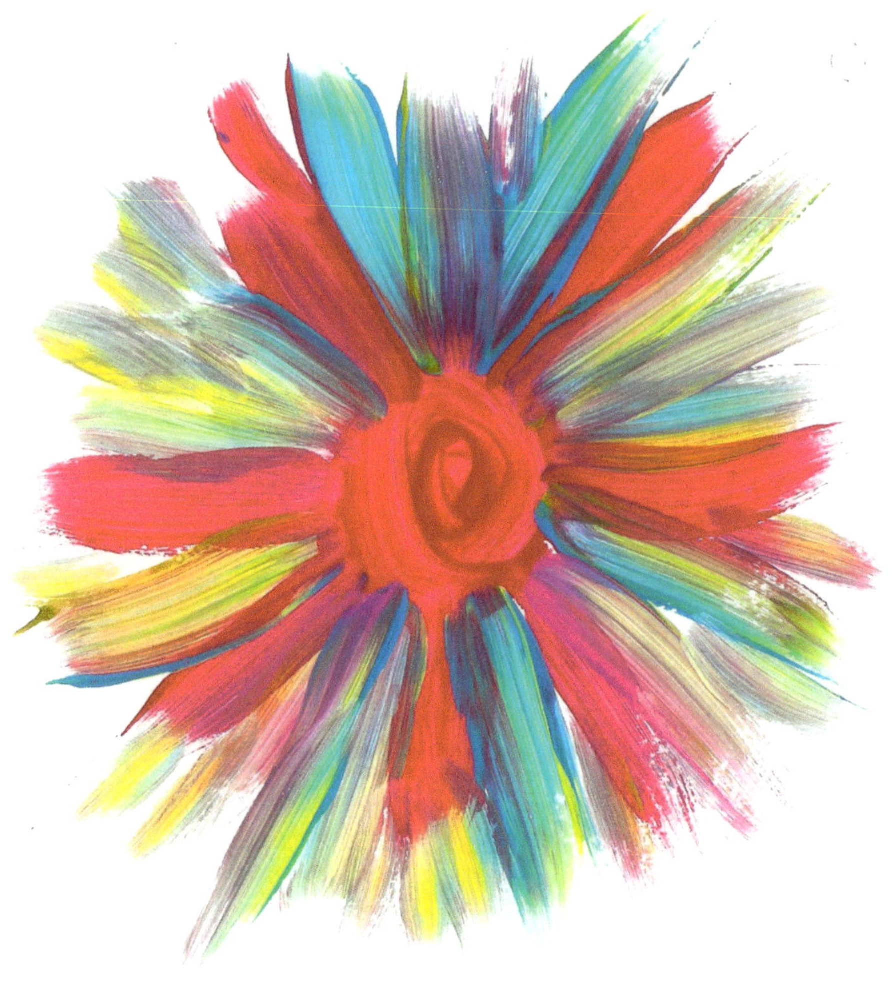

Joyous Explosion of Color

Date completed: July 6th, 2015

Candy painted this after the 4th of July. It does look like a Joyous Explosion of Color.

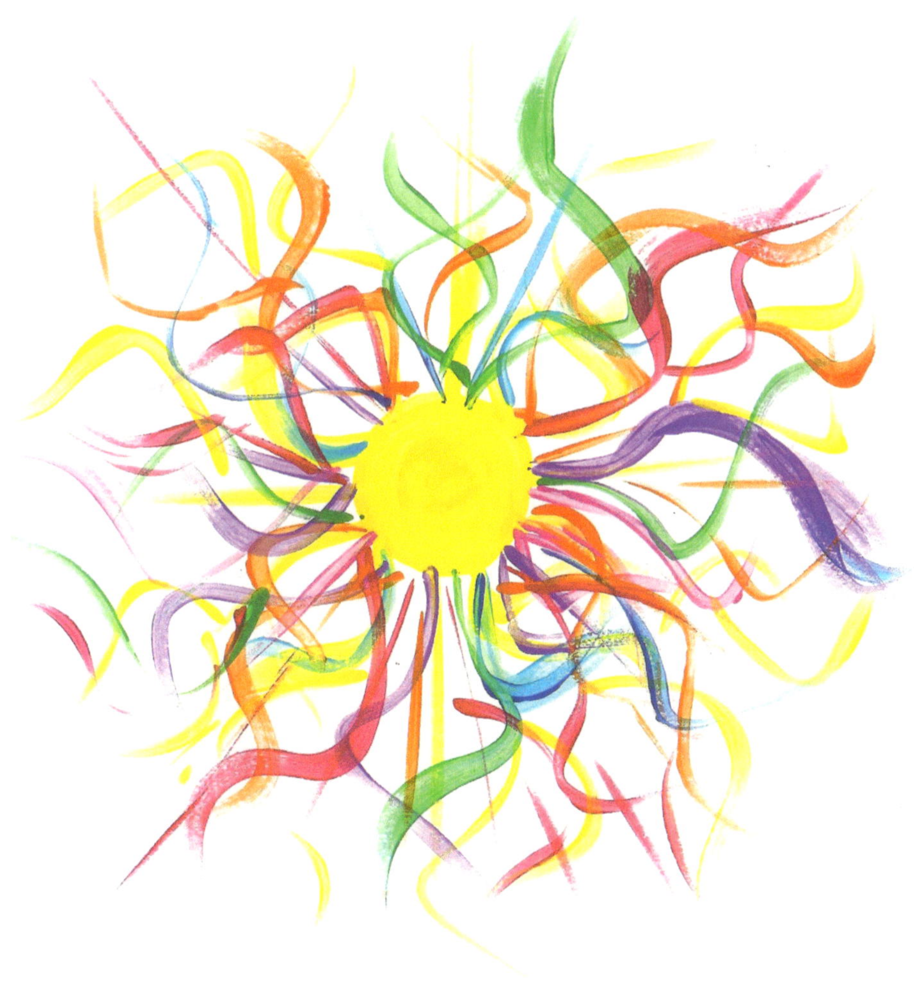

Enlightenment

Date completed: March 25th, 2016

Candy was glowing when she painted this.

APPENDIX

1. To learn more about Candy and her amazing art, here is the link to her Facebook page: facebook.com/candywatersautismartist

2. After her diagnosis, we wrote a song for Candy that we titled "Faith, Love and Hope." It is sung by Jessica Taylor who is from the singing group "The Platters." "Faith, Love and Hope" has become an anthem for autism awareness and has garnered praise from President and First Lady George W. and Laura Bush, President Barack Obama and Secretary of State Hillary Rodham Clinton. Here is the link to the song, words and music copyrighted by Robert & Sandy Waters: https://www.youtube.com/watch?v=kNec1apjFAg

3. On a mission to empower other parents that have a child who has autism with knowledge, we created an Autism Awareness Radio Show titled "The Candy Store" on Blog Talk Radio named after our daughter Candy. In one of our interviews our guest Dr. Sarina Grosswald, a researcher and cognitive learning specialist with The David Lynch Foundation, we learned more about Transcendental Meditation (TM) and decided to take TM classes. For that interview and others see The Candy Store archives. Here's the link: blogtalkradio.com/thecandystore

4. In the early 90's one of Robert and Sandy's (Candy's mother and father) songs "You Are The One For Me" caught the attention of ZZ Top's manager Bill Ham. Bill Ham gave the Waters a song contract. Mr. Ham played the song to the movie director David Lynch who wanted the song to be in one of his movies sung by David Bowie. Yet, since Bowie's approach was to write his own material, the song was never recorded. Nowadays David Bowie's tribute bands love the song and perform it in their live shows around the world. Here is the link to the song titled "You Are The One For Me" Words and Music Copyrighted by Robert & Sandy Waters: https://www.youtube.com/watch?v=W6SZRNa3OB4

5. Candy has always loved music; as she paints she listens to "The Beatles."

6. If anyone would like to purchase a print of Candy's Art please visit her Zazzle Store. Zazzle ships around the World. Here is the link to Candy's Zazzle Store: www.zazzle.com/candace69/product

CANDY'S FANS SPEAK

Katie S. ~ Candy you are an amazing young lady. Your paintings are so full of life and color. Please never stop! This is your God given talent! Every painting I have seen has just made me so happy!

Susan M. ~ I live in Rhinebeck, NY. Rhinebeck is about an hour and a half north of NYC. We are right on the Hudson River with the Catskill Mountains to the West and the Berkshire Mountains to the East. I'm a pharmacist and also make handcrafted soap as a hobby. Your wonderful colors give me inspiration designing my soaps! Thank you Candy!

Jennie M. ~ I have two children both on the spectrum and Candy is such an inspiration to my daughter who longs to be an author (she has ADHD, ASD and complex dyslexia).

Terri B. ~ Hi Candy! I live in Arnold, Mo. USA. I have 2 kids my daughter Sarah is 12 and is in 6th grade and playes the Clarinet. My son Jimmy is 22 and has Autism. He has Aspergars. He graduated high school and now he is writing a Sci-fi Novel. He has 9 chapters finished with 3 sequels. He is very talented like you. Your paintings are amazingly beautiful. They brighten up my day. Thank you for sharing your joy.

Jeanette H. ~ I live in Lisarow on the Central Coast NSW Australia...God's special blessings to you Candy and thank you for sharing your amazing talent and art with us in the land down under..Australia..xx

Helen D. ~ I am from Northampton,Pa...love the vibrant use of colors and the emotion that is evident in the art...beauty is expressed by Candy!!!

Melissa T. ~ I have a 5 yr old cousin with Autism. He's awesome. Thank you for helping to raise awareness.

Bree N Joey G. ~ Amazing energy Candy very inspiring & beautiful. I'm in Ogden, Utah USA.

Barbara N. ~ What beautiful artwork you create, Candy!! My best friend when growing up was named Candy...My Grandson is 7 yrs. old and is Autistic. Please share more pictures!!!

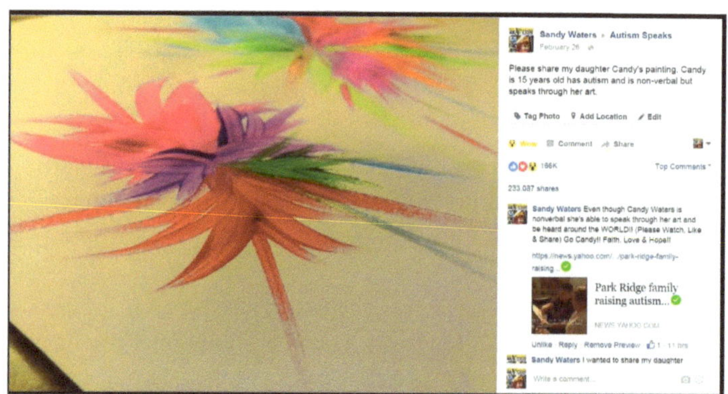

One of Candy's paintings has gone "Viral" on Facebook and is being shared around the World!

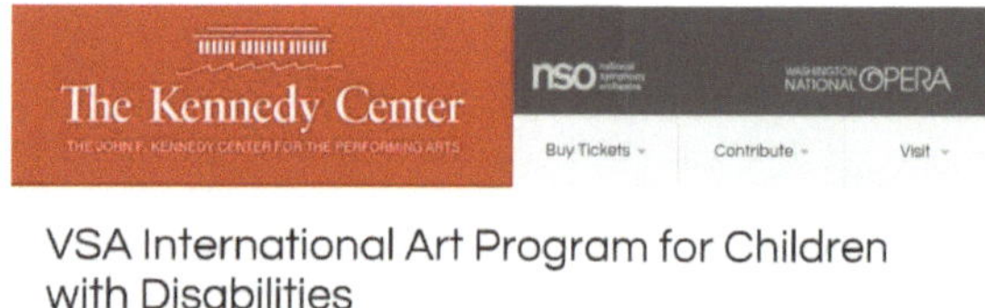

VSA International Art Program for Children with Disabilities
A Jean Kennedy Smith Arts and Disability Program

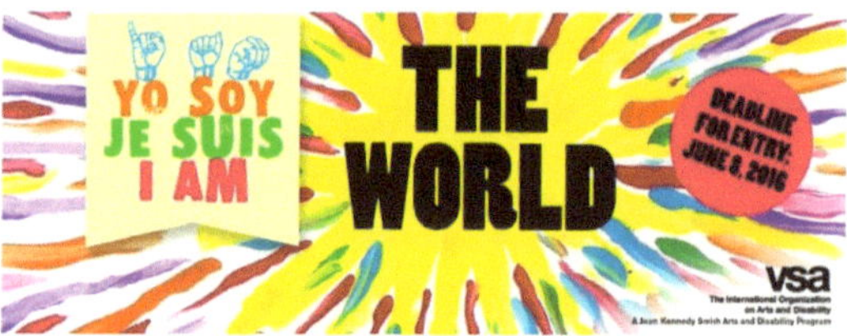

The Office of VSA and Accessibility, a Jean Kennedy Smith Arts and Disability Program of the John F. Kennedy Center for the Performing Arts, proudly presents an exciting opportunity for children with disabilities from around the world to display their

"Jean Kennedy Smith Arts and Disability Program of the John F. Kennedy Center for the Performing Arts" is using Candy's "Radiance" painting for their website. This is such an honor.

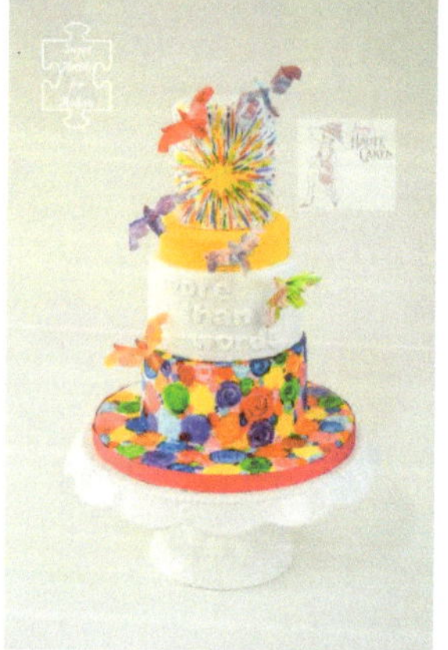

"Sugar Art for Autism" coordinated by Dina Nakad is a collaboration of international cake artists who came together to bring awareness to autism and have used Candy's Artwork as their profile picture on Facebook. One of the cake artists, Jennifer Jenkins Kennedy, has created Candy's Art Cake pictured here."

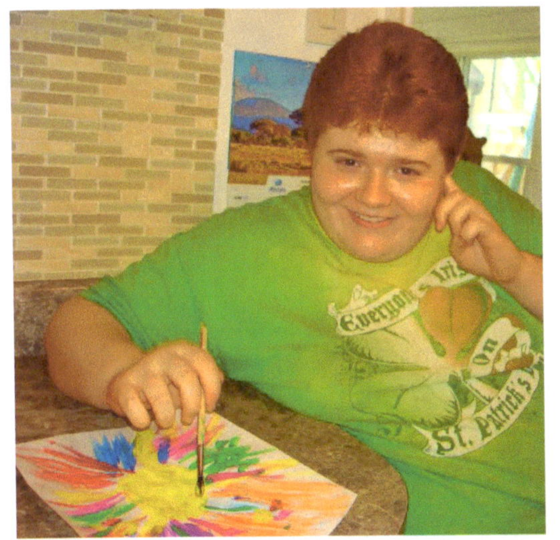

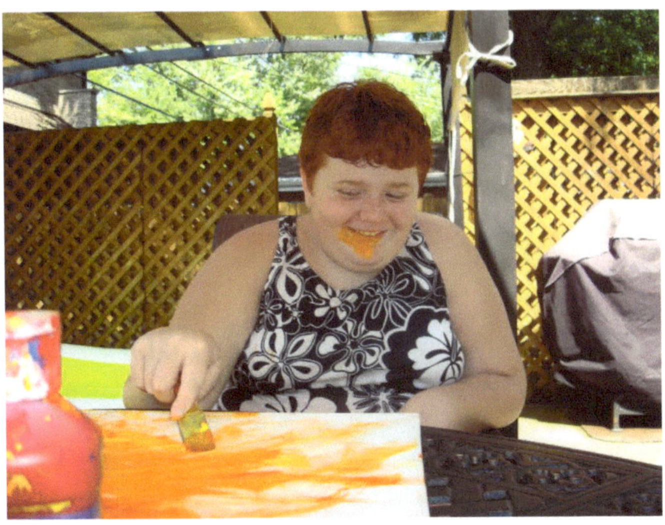

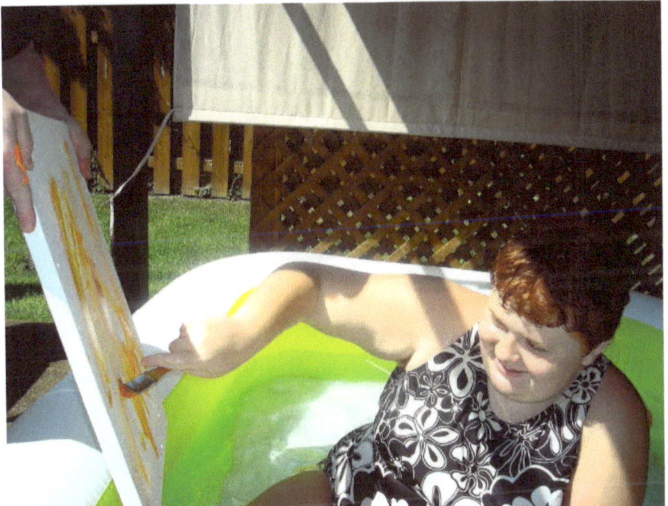

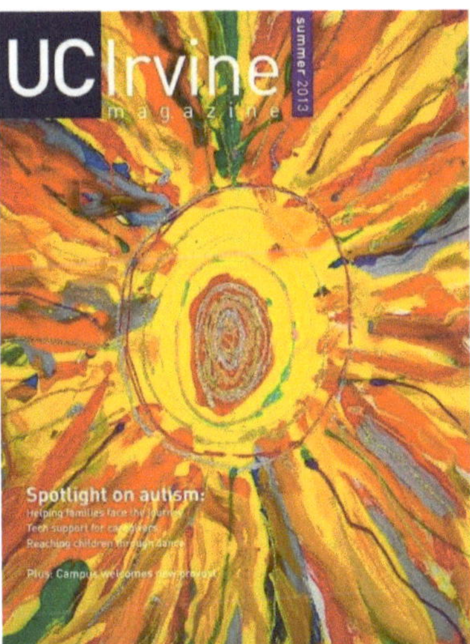

Candy's "Mr. Sun" painting on the cover of The University of California, Irvine Magazine 2013 Summer Issue

ACKNOWLEDGEMENTS

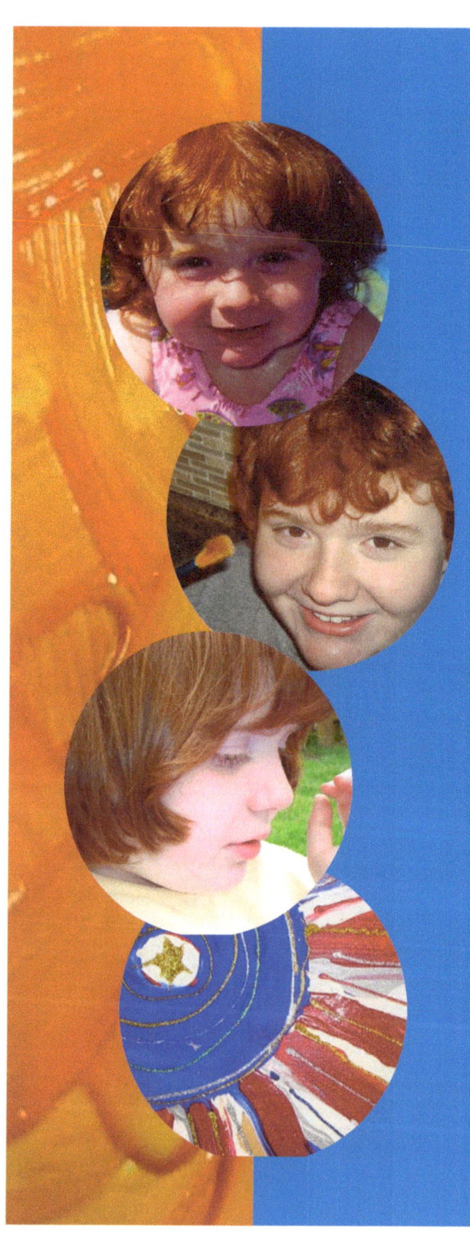

We are grateful to The David Lynch Foundation for helping us learn Transcendental Meditation (TM), David Lynch and Executive Director Bob Roth. There are no words to describe the good work that this foundation does in its mission to reach out to people who live with stress. For us our mission now is to reach out to others who are living with the stress of autism. This includes parents, caregivers or people on the autism spectrum as well. Many thanks to all of our TM teachers Chris and Julia Busch, Carol and Paul Morehead, David Weisman and Carla Brown who made learning TM fun for us. Thank you to Dr. Sarina Grosswald for opening that door for us. In addition we would like to thank Carl and Mary Waters, Candy's grandparents, for all of their love and support. Also, thank you to Autism Speaks for helping our family and many other families that have a child with autism.

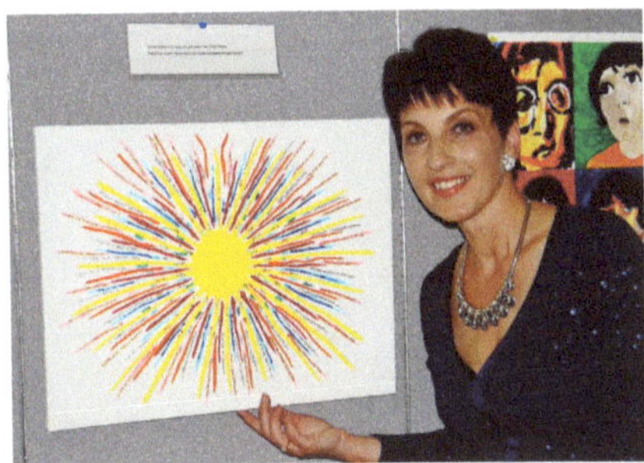

Anna Kennedy OBE (Officer of the Order of the British Empire), Autism Mum & Activist

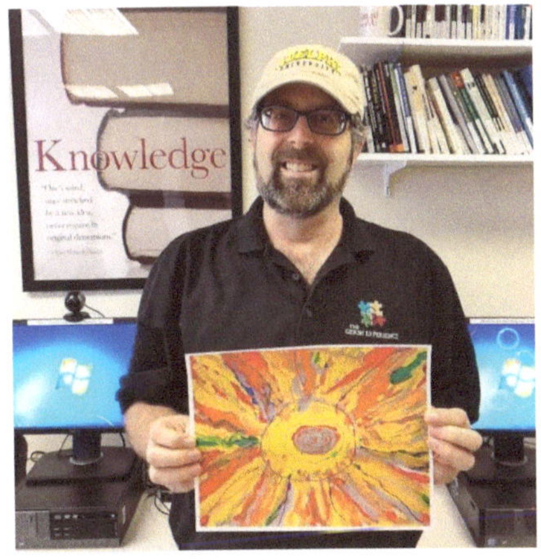

Dr. Stephen Mark Shore ~ Member of the Board of Directors at Autism Speaks & Author

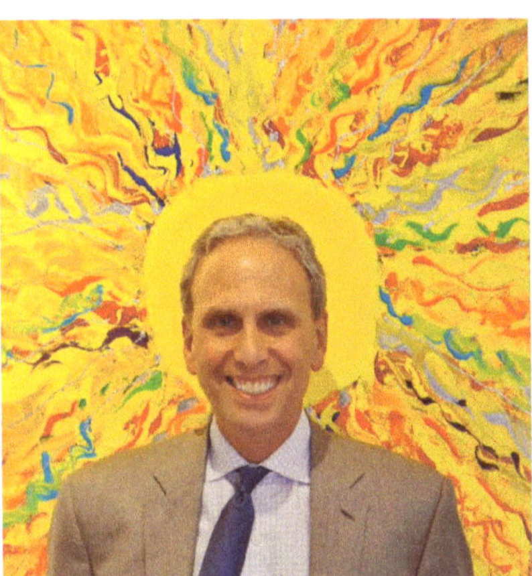

Bob Roth ~ Executive Director of The David Lynch Foundation posing in front of Candy's "Pure Consciousness" painting which is prominently displayed at The David Lynch Foundation Main Office in New York City.

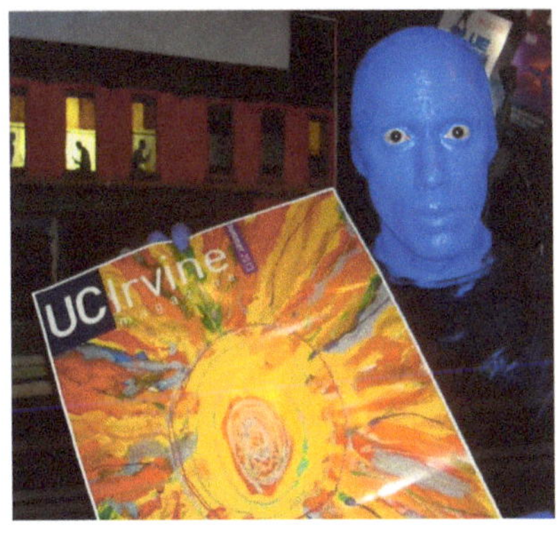

Blue Man ~ From the Blue Man Group

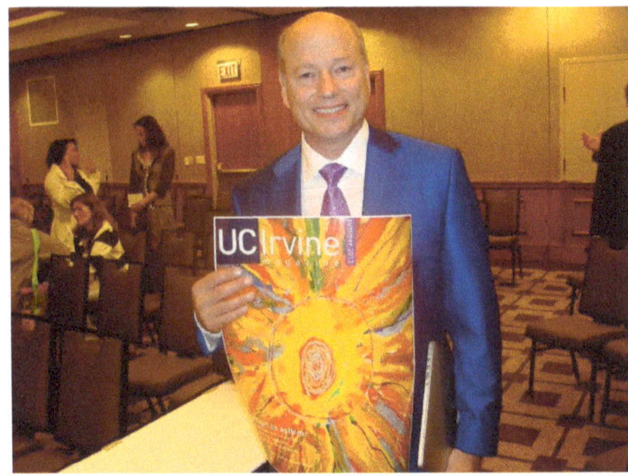

Dr. John Hagelin ~ President of The David Lynch Foundation

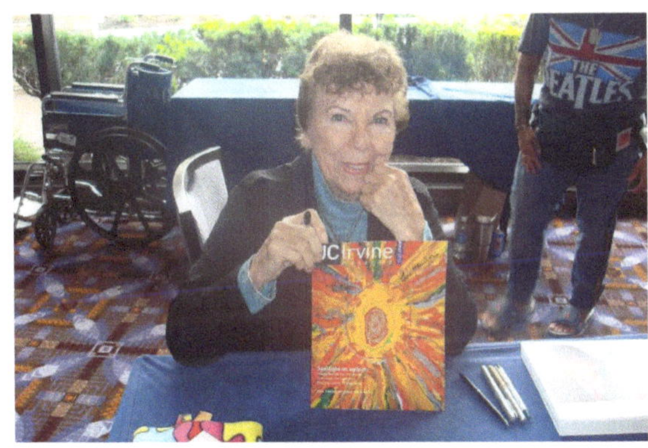

Louise Harrison ~ Beatle George Harrison's Sister

Candy's Famous Fans

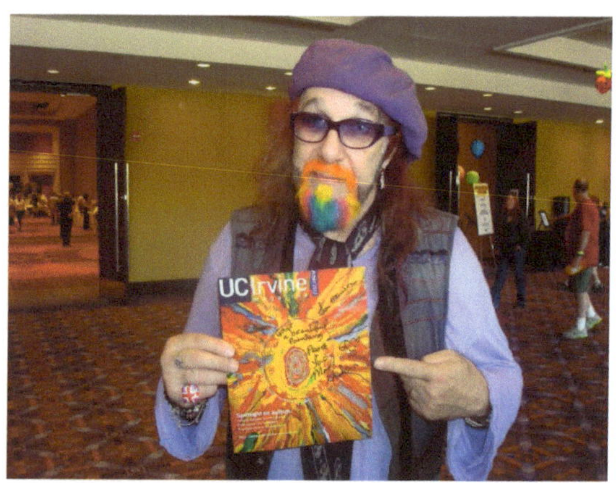

Mark Hudson ~ Record Producer, Musician & Songwriter

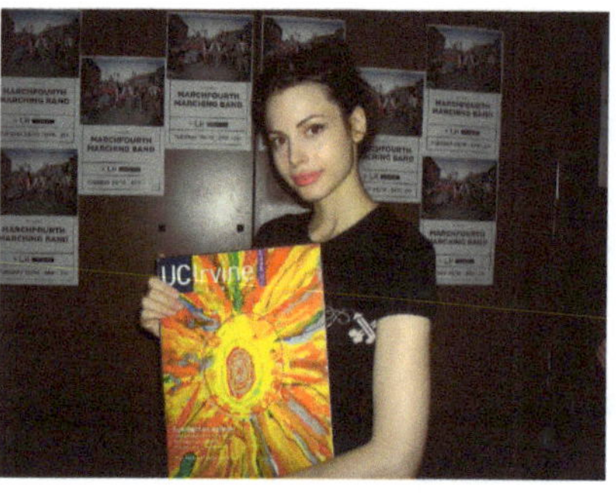

Charlotte Kemp Muhl ~ Model, Singer and member of Sean Lennon's Band "The GOASTT". Charlotte is also Sean Lennon's girlfriend. Sean Lennon is the son of Beatle John Lennon.

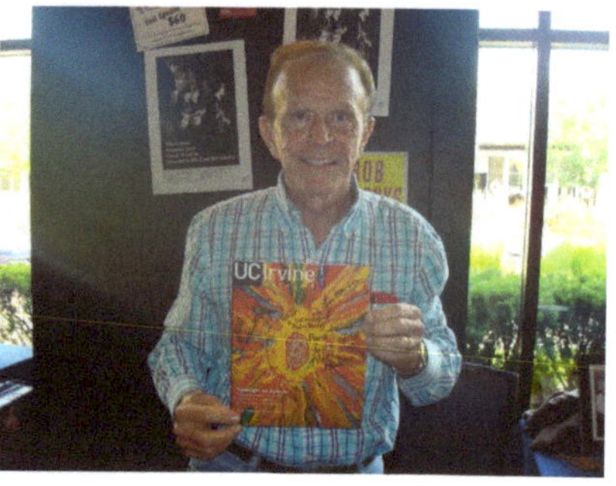

Bob Eubanks ~ The Newlywed Game Show Host

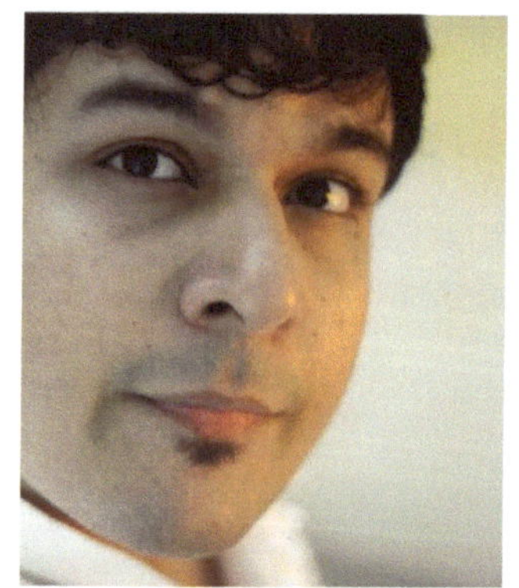

Archan Nair ~ Famous Artist from India

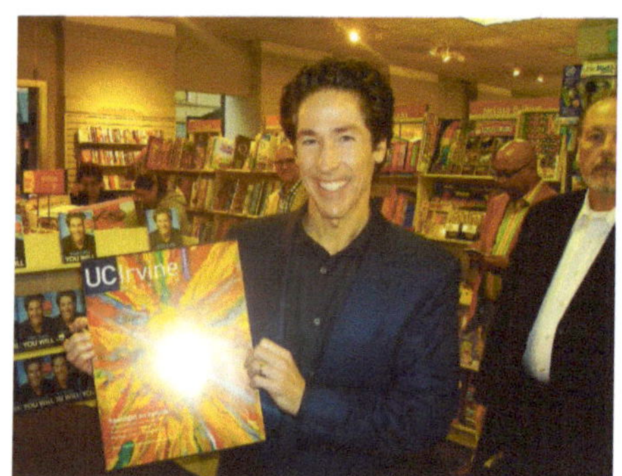

Joel Osteen ~ Preacher

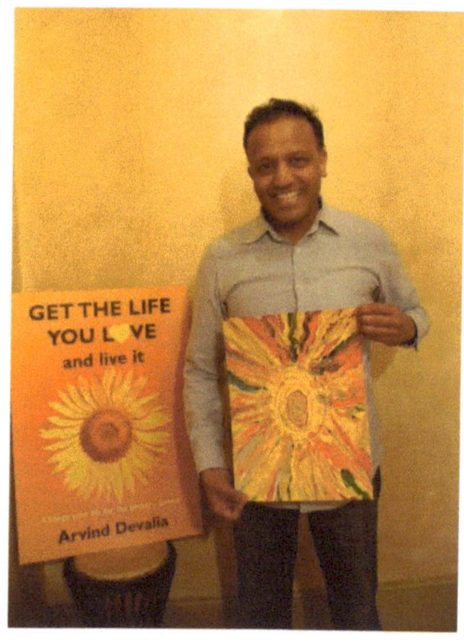

Arvind Devalia ~ Peace Activist, Transformational Coach, Speaker and Best-selling Author of "Get The Life You Love

Candy's Famous Fans

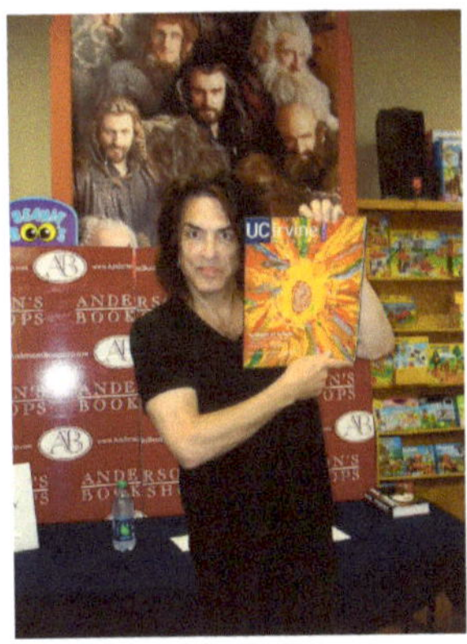

Paul Stanley ~ Rock and
Roll Hall of Fame Member
from the rock band Kiss

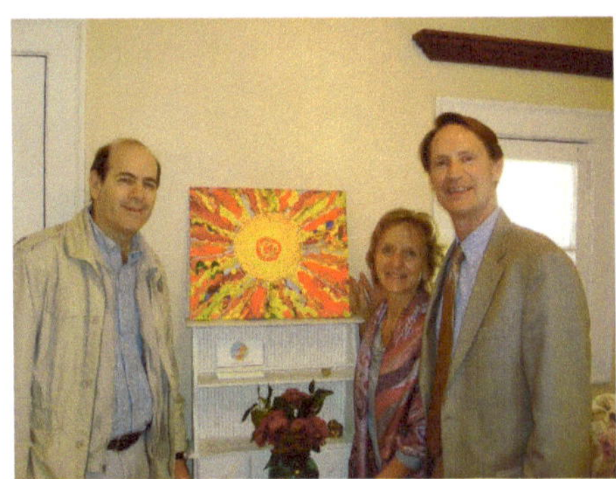

David Weisman, Paul & Carol Morehead ~
Transcendental Meditation Teachers posing with
Candy's Sun painting prominently displayed in the
Evanston, Illinois Transcendental Meditation Center

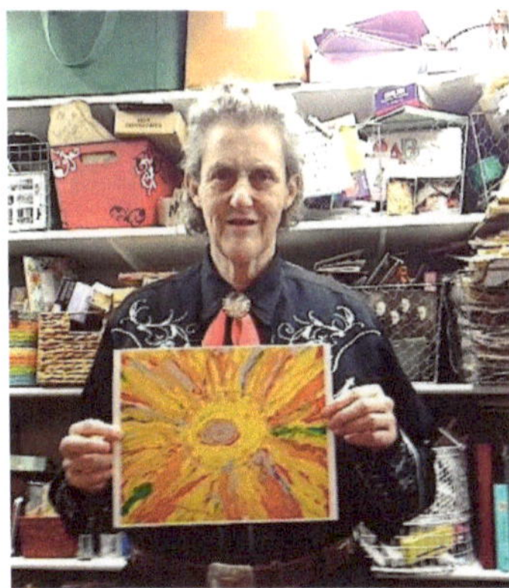

Dr. Temple Grandin ~ Famous
Person with Autism, Author &
Speaker

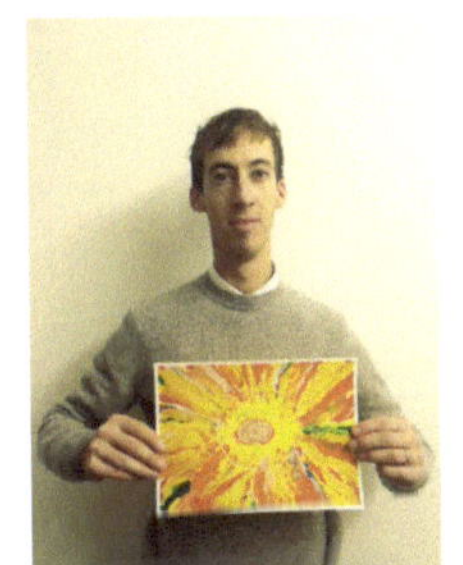

Jean Jullien ~ Famous French Artist who
created the Peace for Paris Symbol

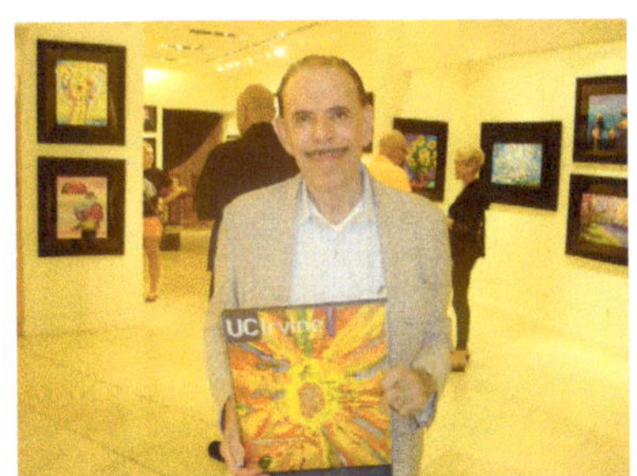

Peter Max ~ Famous Artist

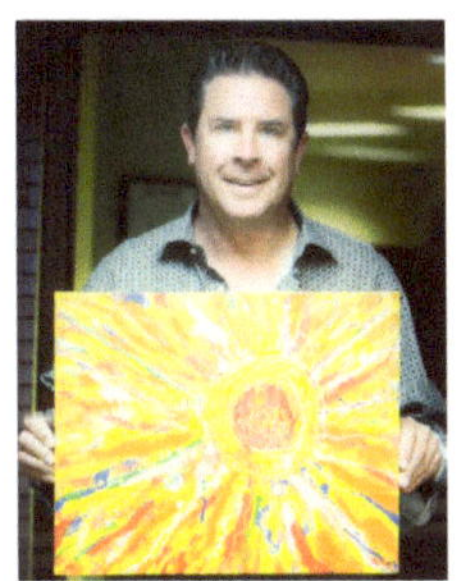

Dan Marino ~ Football Hall
of Fame Great

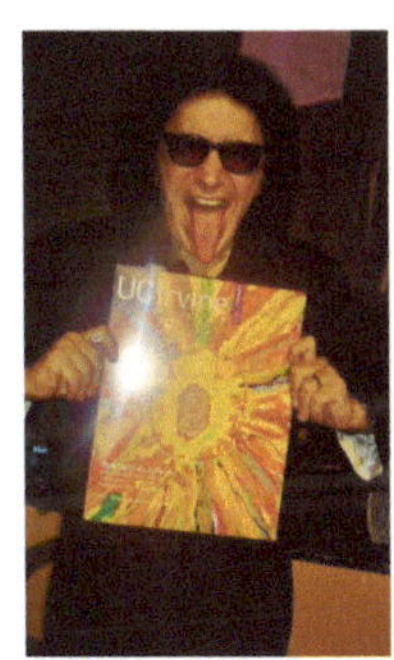

Gene Simmons ~
Rock and Roll
Hall of Fame
Member from the
rock band Kiss

Candy's Famous Fans

Candy's Famous Fans

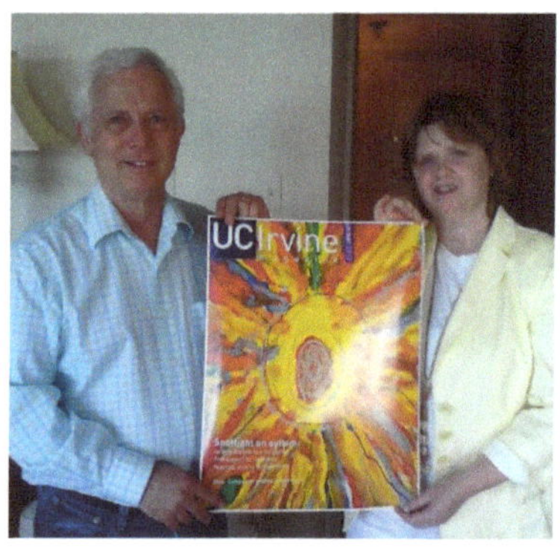

Chris and Julia Busch ~ Regional Directors of Development and Expansion at The David Lynch Foundation

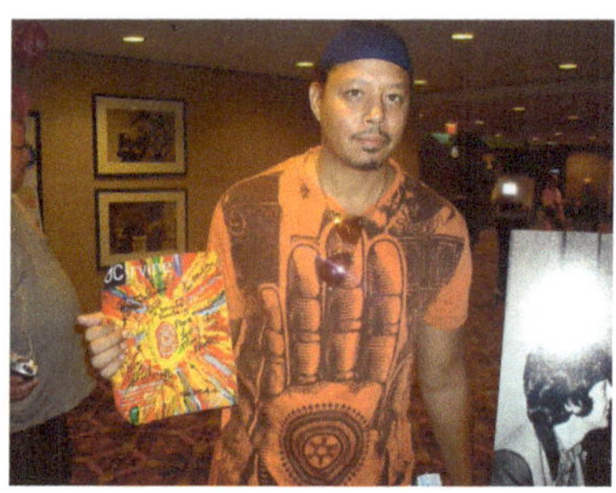

Academy Award Nominated Actor Terrence Howard

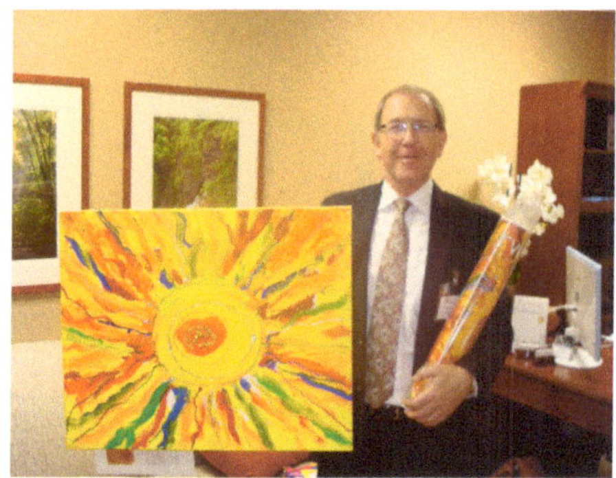

Jim Anderson ~ Transcendental Meditation Teacher posing with Candy's Sun painting that is prominently displayed at the Downtown Chicago Transcendental Meditation Center.

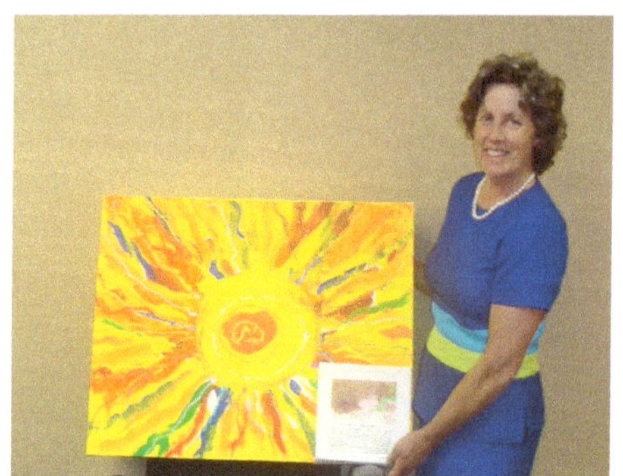

Sara Anderson ~ Transcendental Meditation Teacher posing with Candy's Sun painting that is prominently displayed at the Downtown Chicago Transcendental Meditation Center.

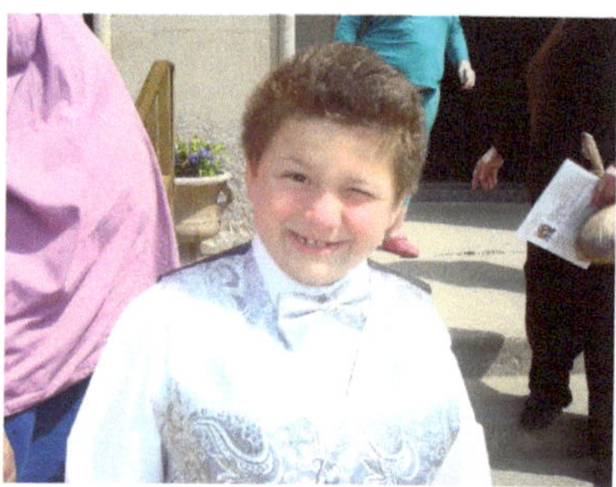

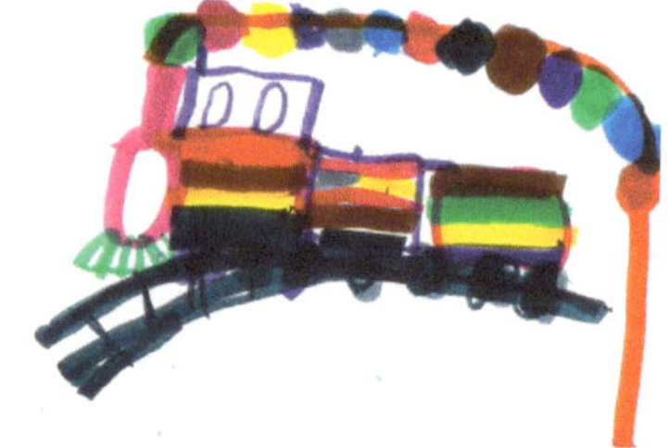

Evan Waters is Candy's younger brother and an artist in his own right. Evan is also on the autism spectrum. Also, here is a drawing of a train that Evan drew.

Here is the link to Evan's Facebook Like Page.
https://www.facebook.com/evanwatersartist

Candy's Famous Fans Speak

"Candy Waters art is a wonderful example of the many talents that young people living with autism share. This is something we celebrate every day at The Marino Campus." ~Dan Marino, Football Hall of Fame Member & Chairman of the Board of The Dan Marino Foundation

"Artist Candy Waters is a very talented young artist who has autism. Her art is very powerful. Candy's art seems very genuine to me, very instinctive and sincere. There's a lot of energy, it's very communicative." ~ Jean Jullien ~ Famous French Artist who created the Peace for Paris Symbol

"Candy's artwork has imaginative bursts of bright happy colors." ~Dr. Temple Grandin ~ Famous Person with Autism, Author & Speaker

"Candy's wonderful art book is a superb testimony to the incredible power of the human spirit! We are all blessed with talent which largely remains untapped – so it's really heartening to see young Candy living a life of no barriers and sharing her gifts with the world.

Her art is truly a gift for all us – and through her huge heart, the divine is teaching us that regardless of where we are in life and no matter what our personal circumstance are, LOVE is all that really matters." ~Arvind Devalia ~ Peace Activist, Transformational Coach, Speaker and Best-selling Author of "Get The Life You Love

"Candy is so amazing! She is so gifted and has an incredible spirit that I can truly feel through her paintings." ~Archan Nair ~ Famous Artist from India

"We Love Candy and her Art at The David Lynch Foundation." ~Bob Roth ~ Executive Director of The David Lynch Foundation

"Candy's artwork is a shining example of the amazing potential of individuals on the autism spectrum. Our job is to find that potential for empowering those with autism to lead fulfilling and productive lives to the greatest extent possible – just like everyone else." ~Dr. Stephen Mark Shore ~ Member of the Board of Directors at Autism Speaks & Author

"Candy Waters art book is yet another example of the talent that lies within the untapped minds of those who live with autism. Candy's art is her unspoken gift to all of us." ~Joe Mantegna ~ Actor

"So many people with autism have amazing abilities and are very creative. Candy Waters and her art is a great example of the remarkable talent and accomplishments that people with autism can achieve.

The David Lynch Foundation is dedicated to bringing the evidence-based Transcendental Meditation technique to children and adults with autism—as well their families—to help them overcome stress and to become happier, healthier and even more creative." ~David Lynch ~ Movie Director

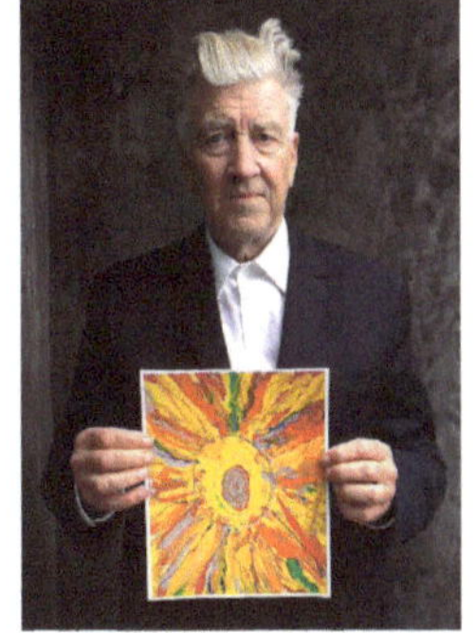

David Lynch ~ Movie Director

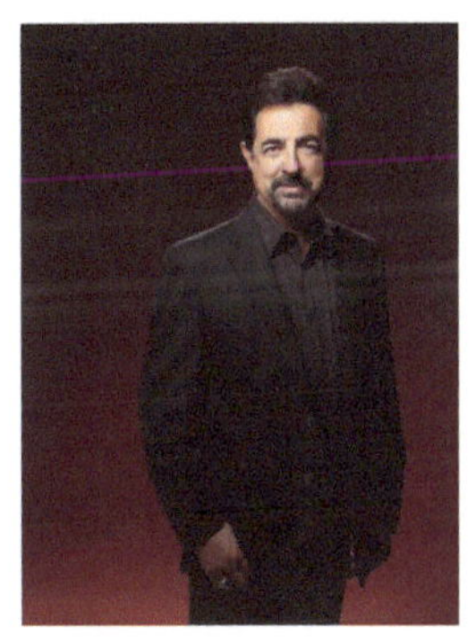

Joe Mantegna ~ Actor

Unspoken Gift

Candy Waters Autism Artist